Straighten Your
Crown

TRISH BLACKWELL

Dedication

To all the daughters of the King, may this book remind you of who you are: beautiful, seen, and loved.

Contents

Foreword

Everything in my life looked ideal. I had my health and wonderful friends and the means to travel (which I was doing a lot of). I was also an executive producer on a feature film about my life called Miss Virginia. As a single, low-income mother in Washington D.C. in the 1990s, I had started a movement to demand better schooling options for the children of our nation's Capital—and won. Now, Hollywood wanted to tell my story.

All through the spring of 2019, the movie team sent "dailies" to me from the set. I watched them and sent back my feedback or approval. I had to pinch myself after watching the performances of Hollywood elites such as Uzo Aduba, Matthew Modine and Vanessa Williams, wondering: Was this really all happening—and to me?

I expected to feel the joy and excitement during the process of telling my story to the world, but what I hadn't expected was the unrelenting feeling of doubt and self-consciousness.

I wondered: Will people like this movie? Will people care? Do I deserve to have a film made about my story?

I quipped to my publicist that I wished the movie had a different name. Flabbergasted, she replied: "But... this film is about YOU."

At times, these feelings of self-doubt overwhelmed me. I withdrew from social activities and when people asked me about the movie, I brushed it off like it was "no big deal". I wanted to feel empowered, to feel happy, to feel like my story mattered, but my brain kept reminding me of all the ways I felt inadequate or undeserving. I prayed about it. I asked the

7

Lord to give me the strength and confidence to tell my story so that others could feel empowered. I prayed for joy, instead of doubt, for confidence, instead of self-criticism.

It was during this time that I began working with Trish Blackwell. We started meeting weekly on video chats and through her confidence coaching, she began infusing my thinking with confidence and joy. We talked through my feelings of self-doubt, we prayed together, and she set me up with exercises to do on my own. In Trish, I found peace and instant camaraderie — a fellow Sister in Christ who seemed to know exactly how I was feeling, and how to help me overcome my negativity.

I arrived at the world premiere of Miss Virginia in New York City, feeling more confident than I had in my entire life. I knew that my prayers for so many years were being answered — and that the Lord had made me a messenger for a story that was going to help other parents, other mothers, just like me.

While that night was special, I was most looking forward to the next premiere event in Washington D.C., where Trish was planning to attend. After six months of "seeing" each other through a screen, I was able to hug the woman who had tapped so expertly into my psyche, who had prayed for and with me, and who had given me the tools to not just face these exciting moments, but to enjoy them. Hugging Trish was like embracing family—she's since become one of my honorary daughters, holding a space in my heart that will remain forever.

Trish is more than a life coach, more than a podcaster, more than a social media influencer. Trish has a gift for spotting the talent and calling in others and helping them reach their greatest potential. She knew my voice needed to be heard, louder than it ever had before, and she helped me realize I was worthy of the attention that needed to accompany that journey. She reminded me often of my calling, of the privilege the Lord had given me in telling my story. She coached me through dark thoughts to a place of true joy.

Trish understands the power of sisterhood in a world that tries to cut us down. She reminds us to make space for each other and that in lifting one another up, we are all elevated. Her confidence coaching comes from a place of genuine belief everyone is worthy of happiness. She believes there is joy in the pursuit of your calling. She believes in God's unconditional love.

In the pages of this book, you will get to know Trish like I do. I know that her words will inspire you, just as they lifted me. I know you will tap into your own purpose and passion as a result. Trish's words are a gift to a troubled world, and I'm forever grateful for what her insight has provided my life. I pray that you can feel that too and then share it with those around you.

Virginia Walden Ford
Filmmaker and Inspiration for the Film Miss Virginia
Author of School Choice: A Legacy to Keep
Social and Educational Activist
https://www.virginiawaldenford.com

INTRODUCTION

Straighten Your Crown

She runs through the palace, hair flowing wildly and beautiful-ly. Emboldened by the privilege of being a princess, she has no cares or concerns. The guards stand at attention as she joyfully twirls by, fully engaged in her imagination and afternoon adventure. She is watched over always. Unconcerned, her steps are light and full of joy.

She knows who she is, the daughter of the king. And so she has no worries, nor fear. She knows who her daddy is, and He rules the kingdom, an excellent king, a trustworthy king, an eternal king. She knows she is cherished and protected. She can be exactly who she is because she is unafraid. Everything she needs will be provided for, and she knows she is part of a royal legacy. Her inheritance is sure, and exceedingly large. She is blessed and highly favored. So she pirouettes through the palace with pleasure across her face, losing herself in her own joy.

Her crown needs straightening because she runs with abandon. It slides off to the side of her head as she spins. She skids across the gold-flaked marble floors to a graceful stop, hesitating for a moment before she opens the heavy doors to the throne room. She enters, running toward her father, who stands up from his throne when he sees her enter. He steps toward her, extends his arms, and kneels down to her level. Adjusting her crown, now tilted to the side, he smiles at her with delight and pride.

She is you.

She is you after you read this book and you understand you are royalty. You are a daughter of the King. He is a powerful king and an almighty king, and He slows down for you. You make Him smile. He wants to spend time with you. He *delights* in you.

Right now, though, it's okay if your crown needs straightening for another reason.

Mine did.

My crown was crooked because my head was downcast. I felt overlooked and behind. I was anxious about my future and never felt like I belonged anywhere.

I didn't even *know* I had a crown. Or an inheritance. And I didn't know that God *delighted* in me and over me. I mean, I knew He loved me—I grew up in Sunday School and with Vacation Bible School songs. But, delight? That's like love on a whole new level—a level I felt unworthy of and very far from. And inheritance? That only existed for the lucky trust fund babies I knew, and I wasn't one of them.

I lived most of my life as a Christian, but I never *felt* like a child of God. I was missing the full life that Christ gave us. I read about it in the Bible, but I just couldn't figure out how to apply it to my life. I couldn't figure out how to stop getting in my own way and to believe that I was who God said I was.

It turns out, the core of the problem was that I didn't think God really loved me, the way a king would love his princess. That felt too ridiculous to be true.

God has stirred me up, spun me around, and sent me to this place—a conversation with you to help you discover your crown. It is an invitation to see that God doesn't just love you from a distance; He delights in being in the details of your life, His child.

This book is a bridge between distance and delight. As you read, you will walk across the bridge with me, discovering, as you reflect on your own life, that all along the way, God has seen you and been with you in ways you never imagined.

When we finally see that God sees us, that He slows down for us, and that He leans in toward us, then the rest of the pressures we have felt fade away. No longer do we have anything to prove. No longer do we have anything to lose. No longer do we need to wonder if we fit and where we belong.

The concept of delight never once crossed my mind until a few years ago as this book was brewing in my heart. God blew the word into my heart like a fresh wind. It stirred me. It woke my soul up, and I became obsessed with following its trail, desperate to feel different from my state of stressed-out, overwhelmed, and modern living.

At first, the concept of delight seemed too slow and too utopian. It seemed too intangible and dainty. To be quite honest, it didn't interest me. It seemed a lot like putting the cart before the horse. I believed delight was a thing I could enjoy in my retirement once I had earned the right to relax and just be. First, though, I needed to prove myself, grow my business, and do something important. Then, I convinced myself, then I would taste that deep soul satisfaction that I was craving.

With two books under my belt, and two toddlers spilling food on my laptop, I felt stuck. I had so much to say, and yet nothing came out. A million book ideas came and went, and nothing felt just right. I shelved the idea of my next book, which was no idea at all, and told myself that I would write when I knew it was the right topic.

Months passed, and I was uninspired. It occurred to me it was time to do something I should have done years prior—talk to God about the book. I prayed and fasted for ten days, hoping to receive some clarity and creativity. On the very last day of the fast, I went to bed without any answers.

I woke in the middle of the night with total clarity. The concept of delight dropped into my heart. It didn't thrill me. I convinced myself that I was simply feeling hazy from the fast, and turned back to sleep, certain I wouldn't remember the next day. *No thanks, Lord.* Please have one of my more spiritual and sane sisters write this. *Give me something easier, something I understand, and that I won't fumble over.*

But I couldn't shake it. It was like a little hitchhiker thistle that caught hold of my heart. Tiny as it was, it was all I could think about, and it poked in just the right spots. It bothered me just enough to dig down and pay attention. The word *delight* had a magnetic pull on my heart. God was unveiling more and more about what He wanted me to discover in it every day, yet I still felt so unequivocally unqualified to be writing about it.

I'm not one for spoilers, but since you are holding this book in your hands, you know that, against all odds, I ended up writing a book about one of the most important concepts in life that I almost missed.

If this book moves you, it is not because of me. It is only because of God. He has taken my jumbled, disjointed, and lacking efforts and woven them together as only He could.

So, what is delight? And how does it get us to that crown?

Delight is the switch that wakes up our hearts to the identity we have as children of God. It wakes us up, reminding us that the things that are unseen are exceedingly more powerful than the things of this world that we can see. It tells us we are loved, and we walk in worthiness because of who we are as God's daughters.

Discovering the delight God has for you is an awakening that will settle your heart in security for the plans He has for you. For me, it took being able to see where God was—where His delight and love were actually present—in my life for me to believe that the plans He has for me were good, trustworthy, and in His hands.

As I have studied delight, I've found that it is the part of our wiring that makes us come most alive. It allows us to engage fully, to awaken exuberance and to feel like we belong.

When I delight in my children, my parental love overflows into palpable joy. When I delight in my work, my fingers dance across the keyboard without thought, stringing together beautiful concepts that flow directly from my heart onto the screen without effort. When I delight in my breath while I run, all self-conscious anxiety and judgment dissipate and peace overflows in my heart. The river of peace trickles down across every fiber of my body, and I feel engulfed in love and beauty. I feel alive enough and desired all at one time. And for a girl who spent half her life hating her body, wishing her quirks away, and working obsessively to feel loved, that is a miracle. It is an answer to everything I have ever wanted, but in the absolute opposite way I thought I would ever get it.

Delight is our emotional permission slip to settle into the present moment God has given us and to rest alongside streams of still waters. It is our access pass to feeling enough.

The following chapters of this book are a treasure map I want to share with you. They result from my exploration of delight that unexpectedly ended in riches beyond my wildest expectations. I want to invite you on this adventure with me.

My husband, Brandon, is a hero at the beach. He digs holes, builds castles, plays pirate, and buries treasure. Our kids come alive with the mystery, the clues, and the excitement of seeing where the adventure he's created will take them. In the same way my kids have done dozens of times at the beach, we find the treasure where X marks the spot. This book will help you string together clues of God's delight in your life to help you discover where to settle in and claim your inheritance and position.

So, let's take this map by its corners and figure out how to find the treasure. Your map will differ from mine, but I hope that in sharing my pursuit, you'll be inspired to look in all corners, under every rock, and into all kinds of unfamiliar terrain to find yours.

As I started bushwhacking the brush in my life, looking for the treasures buried in delight, I didn't know what I would discover, or what I was really even looking for. It feels off-putting, when you start on this adventure, because you are looking for something that you aren't yet sure of. That's okay. Press on.

Here's what I can tell you. When you see it, you will know it. When you feel it, it will be clear. When you taste it, your heart will come alive. You will know your treasure—the crown that comes with being a child of the King—when you get close to it. It will feel like love. It will feel like belonging. It will feel like peace about the future that you have never tasted.

The clues on your map won't be in the same order as mine. But press on. They're all there, waiting to be discovered. I lay the chapters of this book in the order that they happened in my own life. As you read you will see each chapter address a topic of life commonly experienced, helping you see God's love and faithfulness show up in both the good and the bad. Each chapter will help you look at an area of your life through a new lens, one that reveals where God's delight shows up in places you never would have expected.

My treasure map's first clue started with a sound. I heard a whisper of delight in the wind while standing in a valley in Scotland. There was something unusually familiar about it, but wild too. You'll hear more about what awoke me to my first moment of conscious delight in the first chapter, but for now, I can tell you, it confused me. Peace swept over the pressure I felt in my heart, and joy took the place of anxiety. I experienced a moment of spiritual euphoria, or what I could only otherwise describe as the tangible love of God.

That first clue felt like a hug from God. The wind whipped around me, swirling and circling, wrapping itself around me. It heard it and I felt it. I couldn't see it, and I had no words for it, but I knew something had shifted.

It has taken a year of research for me to follow this treasure map. It turns out, God had been showering my life with clues of delight for years. The clues sprinkled every turn of my life; I had just been too busy to notice them.

As you read this book, you'll see delight in places you expect, like childhood memories, beautiful sunsets, and big life moments. But you will find delight even more in the places you might not expect, like in the mundane moments, in conflict, and in disappointment. Delight dwells in every crevice of our lives, even the darkest ones.

I discovered that in those dark seasons—the ones where I felt abandoned, where I was broken, and where my life felt like it was hanging on by a thread—delight was there too. In big ways. Through prayer, journaling and therapy, God healed my vision. He rewrote my memories and gave me sight to see old memories with fresh eyes.

It is my hope and prayer that as I share some of these revelations of delight, you too will peel back the veil in your life to see things differently than you might have thought they were. As we pull out our treasure maps and embark upon the quest for delight, be encouraged, this fortune is not scarce or reserved for someone other than you.

In fact, He promised it to us.[1] We are told that God will delight in us with gladness, and that with His love, He will calm all of our fears. But the Bible doesn't stop there. God's delight in us compels Him to be a mighty savior, to live among us and to rejoice over us—yes, sing over us with delight—with joyful songs.[2]

My prayer is that this book is a map that takes you to a place of beauty, a peaceful place where you feel loved, you know your purpose, and you can hear the songs of joy and shout of delight that God sings over you. He loves you with tenderness and intimacy and will quiet you with his love. But relax; take the pressure off yourself. This is an adventure after all, and adventures are fun. So, as I share on the following pages some treasures I have discovered, get ready to see things in your life and your memories through a new lens, the lens of delight.

As with any adventure, delight is mysterious—and inviting. So, lean in closer, friend, for an adventure of self-discovery and deep love awaits.

CHAPTER 1

Discovering Delight in the Quiet Places

I spent most of my childhood at a pool. My memories float through my mind, always taking me back to car rides on the way to swim practice, practice drills, or hours on end spent on the deck at swim meets. When I wasn't swimming for sport, I spent my time either playing at our local pools, lifeguarding, or teaching swim lessons.

In what feels like millions of hours of memories around the pool deck, one stands out: playing telephone on the pool deck with my girlfriends. We would sit on the concrete deck in a circle, goggles twirling in hand, delighted that we had time to play.

If you've never played telephone before, the game is simple. One person starts by thinking of a secret or something funny they want to share. That person leans over and quietly whispers the secret into the ear of the person beside them. You're only allowed to repeat it one time. The recipient of the whisper then passes the secret in a whisper to the next girl beside her. This whisper passing continues until the last girl in the circle hears the secret and gets to say it out loud to the group.

Without fail, it's never anywhere close to what was first said. Everyone laughs and feels closer together.

Whispering does that. It draws us close in intimacy with one another. It solidifies friendships and it piques curiosities.

God whispers to us. He whispers to you, and He whispers to me. Like any whisper, we need to pay attention to it to hear it. Lean in and get close—you don't want to miss what He says.

I haven't always been able to hear God. My life has felt much like the game of telephone. I often have felt like I was doing life wrong and mishearing what God wanted for me and from me. But one day I heard a whisper that changed my life.

The story starts in a beautiful place on a windy day. God whispered, but I didn't hear Him at first. I didn't hear Him because I wasn't expecting to meet with Him. I wasn't looking for Him.

It turns out that God likes unplanned meetings. Or maybe it's that they seem unexpected to us, but not to Him. He's been trying to get our attention all along. He has been chasing us with whispers, showing up in small ways until we finally see Him for the first time in a way that stops us.

When you finally hear the quiet of His voice calling, it feels like the world stops for a moment and your soul feels at home.

I was in the Scottish Highlands when my world stopped. I had been a Christian my entire life, but in my twenties my faith was fleeting. God felt distant. My heart was heavy, overwhelmed with pain, disappointment, and too many unanswered prayers to think that God still loved me or cared for me.

I still believed in God, and believed He moved and answered prayers, but for other people. *Something is wrong with me*, I thought.

How wrong I was.

God moves everywhere, and He's always speaking to us, if we listen. He whispers to us in the wind, He shows up in the way He paints the sky, and He makes himself known in the gurgles of a newborn. Sometimes, it is hard to hear God's whisper—because we run lives dripping in distraction. But if you pay attention, He is there. And the whisper has purpose, for the whisper draws us near.

A whisper is a mark of intimacy, no matter your age. As a child, the game of telephone helped me determine my core group of friends. As an adult, I whisper to my children. Whispering brings us close; it creates something special between us. It seals us together.

That day in Scotland, God paused the world for me so we could meet through a whisper. It happened when I least expected it, and in a place that I had never intended to visit.

It was September 2010, and I was still spiraling from the assault that turned my life upside down. I was spiritually disinterested. I wanted to be strong on my own and to make sure no one could ever catch me or hurt me again.

I had convinced myself that God had given up on me and that I had disappointed Him. Clinging to my identity as a victim, I was angry at God for allowing such deep hurt in my life. I buried the pain and the abuse of the assault with distraction. I found refuge in being a workaholic during the day—at work and in my workouts— and then drinking with friends to keep from feeling.

To rebuild my fortitude, I picked up endurance running, biking, and swimming. At first the workouts were a way to process my trauma and to help me feel safe. Then they became my life and part of my healing. I soon completed my first marathon, which led to my first Ironman triathlon and a litany of other endurance events.

Eventually, I landed in Edinburgh at the World Championships with Team USA for the Duathlon, an endurance run-bike-run event. I had dreamed for over twenty years of representing my country athletically, and it was a dream come true.

As luck would have it, I had a friend who lived in Scotland. She cheered me on as I ran and biked around Edinburgh. I biked the twisty course with an epic volcanic hill as a backdrop for the competition. After the race, she returned to work, so I filled my time with window-shopping and a day tour on a public tour bus.

I boarded the bus with no expectations. They filled it with tourists, none of whom I remember befriending despite my natural extraversion. Despite the lingering high of finishing such a challenging race, my heart was heavy. I was walking the line between depression and being sadder than I had ever felt. I didn't know who I was, I didn't know where God was, and I didn't trust anyone. The ache in my broken heart felt too heavy to bear and as if it would never go away.

The bus left Glasgow midday and drove the narrow Scottish roads with adept agility. We saw lochs, narrow sea inlets, stopped at local pubs, and some incredible scenery. It was nice. Nice, but not remarkable. That is why nothing could have prepared me for what happened next.

The last stop of the excursion collided with the fall of dusk. Climbing down the steep bus stairs, I lazily stepped out into the field to check out why the tour guide insisted we see and feel in the valley of Glencoe.

That's when something special happened.

The wind changed, and I felt like I got swept up into it.

The other tourists became white noise and seemed to disappear. I followed a small, pebbled footpath toward the sound of a rippling stream. It was dark now, but light from the moon illuminated the volcanic, mossy peaks on opposite sides of the stream's reflection.

I crouched down by the water, reaching in and feeling the crispness wash over my hand and my soul. I might have been there for one minute, or one hour. It's impossible to say because my world paused entirely.

The moment felt sacred. Time stood still, and the wind picked up, swirling around me and moving my hair in a way you only see in a movie.

That wind snaked its way directly into my heart. I felt overcome with peace. And hope descended upon me. In the darkness and obscurity of that place, I felt seen. It was as if all of creation was singing to me—the beauty was entirely surreal and overwhelming. I felt at home, even though I was on the other side of the world from my house.

As I prepared to climb back on the tour bus, I wasn't sure what to do with what I had felt. I just knew that for the first time in years I had hope for the future. I felt safe and loved; I felt at home. I didn't know what I had heard, and I didn't recognize it as the Lord's voice, but I recognized I wanted more of it, whatever it was.

When God whispers and you hear it, you feel at home; you feel confident you're where you're supposed to be. It's a feeling so deep that it can surprise you and frighten you. It feels too good to be true. And so, out of fear that I would never feel it again, I drank in every detail of the greatness that circled around me.

The glacial-sided slopes surrounding me boasted with grandeur. From every angle, peaks surrounded me, like I was in the palm of God's hand. I felt safe, like the chill of the wind somehow surrounded me with a warm embrace. It was the first time I believed I would feel love again. Before Glencoe, my heart was washed up and dried out. But after that night and that whisper, God planted the seed of love and potential for something bigger in my life.

My life transformed after that. It was only a few weeks later that I would find myself on a blind date with a man named Brandon who would become my husband.

Nine years later, when my family and I were creating our itinerary for a trip to the United Kingdom, I struggled to explain to Brandon why Glencoe was so important to include. At the time the memory was powerful, but somewhat vague. An ever-supportive husband, Brandon was happy to add a visit to the valley and the Western Highlands to our plans.

We know Glencoe as one of the most picturesque places in Scotland. When you drive through its valley you feel small, and your heart enlarges from the beauty of the place. It suspends your emotions with an uncanny sense of delightful turmoil. In Glencoe your eyes drink in beauty that your vocabulary can't match. Google it for yourself. You'll find dozens of blogs and articles that say something like, "words just don't describe this beauty," or "pictures don't properly do this beauty justice."

In short, Glencoe is the type of place where you can practically feel God, even if you don't believe in him.

Our trip to Glencoe took us directly across Scotland. Driving on Scottish roads—in a small rental car, on the opposite side of what we're accustomed to—was an entirely unique challenge. The roads are narrow, without shoulders, and windy, requiring total focus and adept control. The highways often edge themselves in between the base of a mountain and the edge of a loch, with such jaw-dropping contrast that it's hard to keep your eyes on the road.

After three hours of driving, I started getting nervous. What if I had over-romanticized Glencoe? I was dragging my husband and young children across the country to see a place I *think* changed my heart. But I wasn't really sure why it was so special or if it was really any different from anywhere else in Scotland.

When the road finally opened up to the bogs that stretch out before the entrance of Glencoe Valley, all of my fears disappeared. It was eerie and awe-inspiring, like entering a movie set where an epic battle scene takes place. I felt joy awaken in my bones as we drove forward into the beauty before us. The scenery was so overwhelmingly beautiful that felt like it hugged my soul.

I convinced Brandon to stop on the side of the road for a quick selfie while the kids remained buckled in their car seats. We had little time that day—the kids were cranky, and we needed to find some dinner and our new Airbnb. It was beautiful, and he agreed, but I longed to have words, to have him feel what I felt when I was there.

Our Airbnb cottage in the Highlands was a short drive past Glencoe. We spent days there, with the cottage as our base camp for our Highlands adventures, like searching for the Loch Ness monsters and having tea parties in old castles.

We planned to have a full-day hike and picnic in the Glencoe Valley, and I was nervous. Hiking with a two-year-old and four-year-old always comes with hiccups.

I woke up anxious the morning of our hike, hoping that my memory of the whispers I felt in Glencoe in 2010 wouldn't disappoint. I had dragged my family across the world to come back to a place where I felt the love of God. It seemed ridiculous and risky. And, when traveling with tired toddlers, it's easy for what should be a perfect day to turn into a disastrous day.

What if it rained? What if we couldn't find a place to park or a trail that my youngest could walk? What if the kids refused to eat the picnic, and we wasted our emotions fighting over food? What if Brandon didn't think the valley was as epic as I did? What if the place really wasn't as special as I thought it was? What if we weren't dressed warm enough, and the kids whined all day? What if I didn't feel God's presence in the same way as I had before?

What if. What if. What if?

Our first stop was a path at the intersection of three waterfalls. They come so close to the road that when you drive through on the highway, you're convinced that you could reach through your car window and touch them. We ambled along in our day, hitting the prime points of the scenic spots, eventually settling our little SUV into a tiny gravel lot on the side of the road by the famous Three Sisters peaks.

We trekked up a single-track trail to find a flat rock ledge for our picnic. I popped open a bottle of champagne, poured it into plastic picnic cups for Brandon and me to share as we both smiled in wonder. We had a full five seconds of bliss before we were both running in opposite directions to chase wandering toddlers and keep them from falling off the jutted terrain drops.

The afternoon of light strolling we had expected turned into proper hiking on treacherous trails with two young children. The hike wasn't perfect. The kids thew alternating tantrums. My two-year-old almost fell off a rock ledge and into a waterfall, and my daughter lost her boot to a mud pit hidden by the overgrown grass-covered slope. Even after being warned by her mud experience, I ended up thigh-deep in a mud pit myself and almost dropped my son headfirst onto a rock.

We were sluggish, sloppy, and seriously happy. It felt like we hiked for hours, but really, we did more side-to-side hiking than straightforward movement, and we ended upon only about fifteen minutes away from our original starting point.

You know those moments in life when you wouldn't change a thing? That day, with all the challenges of "hiking" in the Scottish Highlands with two toddlers, was still a perfect day. My soul was deliriously happy.

We finished the day with one last stop. I wanted to see if we could find the exact place where I had met with God nine years earlier. I needed to find out what actually happened to me there. We piled the tired kids back into the car and took a chance. We dodged some ditches and mud puddles as we navigated the little pull off section with the sunset shining brightly into our eyes.

I stepped out of the car and gasped. It was the same spot from nine years prior. I now know it as Loch Achtriochtan, but I'll never call it that. I'll only refer to it as my spot with God.

We tumbled into the valley, landing next to a stream as the sun fell. The darkness was settling around us like a blanket, streams of light peeking through the surrounding peaks and shining on our feet like beacons of hope.

And that's when I felt it—the same touch of God that I had felt in 2010—and it all came together.

This place, a kaleidoscope of shadows and sunlight, cast a beautiful vision of home. I felt God's whisper once again, pulling me intimately close. The wind blew, and we were thankful for our scarves, tightening them with each whirl of the wind.

The wind spoke to my heart as it swirled around me: *I see you. I am with you. I love you.* And as that whisper came again, it invited me to let go a bit and let the anxiety sitting in the background of my mind fall away. A quiet peace swept over me and I felt a spirit of rejuvenation cover me. It was everything I had been looking for in my life, all in one place.

I hadn't known I was so weary. I didn't realize that even then, in 2019, I was still drinking the water of the world. It's water that makes you weary, fills you with busyness, and keeps you constantly distracted and always behind. My life at the time was beautiful, but I hadn't realized I was carrying a burden, this time with the weariness that comes with feeling like you have so much to do and just never enough time. I was stretched thin and worn out.

Standing there, with my family playing tag in the surrounding stream, I was finally sure that I hadn't imagined what I had felt years before. This place *had* changed me.

This was my place of rebirth—the place where I remembered I belonged with God and that I came home to Him in my heart.

We finished our perfect day and the last bit of champagne, skipping rocks by an isolated white stone cottage so idyllic that it looked set up for a postcard. Before the last light disappeared, the sun dove sharply between the steep mountain edges. Those brilliant streams of remaining light bursting out through the cracks felt personal and purposeful, as if God was reaching out to touch me. As my kids ran circles around the cottage in the setting sun, my heart ran circles around the idea that God really was present in my life.

I stood still, safe, and in the hand of an unquestionably perfect, delightfully detailed God. As we drove home that night, I swam in a sea of stillness. I didn't open email, didn't scroll social media, didn't talk. I just held my glass of wine and stared out the darkened window that overlooked the neighboring loch. Anything I said or did felt like it would cheapen the worshipful state of my soul. I felt the delight of being with God and Him with me—and I didn't want to anything else to distract me.

The quiet is where we drink of the water of life. It doesn't have to be in a Scottish valley or miles away from your home. The quiet is anywhere we can be still long enough to hear a whisper. If you listen closely enough, the whisper in your quiet place will always say the same thing: *I see you. I am with you. I love you.*

Consider what would happen in your life if you heard God say to you, *I see you. I am with you. I love you.* What if this book is that whisper? What if I wrote these pages just for you? I believe that I did.

This collection of stories might not ruffle your hair like a gust of wind in the Scottish Highlands, but it can still wrap itself around your soul, reminding you you're more than you have thought you are. You are loved. You are seen. You are surrounded. You are a child of the King. And that changes everything.

After Glencoe, all wind feels spiritual to me. Its very nature has a divine presence that as innately powerful as it is absolutely invisible. As I write this, I sit in the rocker on my front porch on a windy day in October. The Virginia tree line is bursting into brilliant colors and their limbs wave back and forth from the power of wind that blows. It feels like God is reminding me that, amid my busy week, He cares, He sees, and He is right with me.

On days like this, I open my arms wide and stretch them out as wide as my petite frame can manage. I breathe in, close my eyes, and hug the wind that presses against me. It is a hug from heaven. My kids have seen me do this, and now on windy days you can find them with their arms outstretched, squealing that God is hugging them too.

Those moments immediately transport me back to Glencoe. I feel fully accepted, intricately loved, and flooded with peace. You can have this same peace (and you don't have to travel across the ocean to find it). When you are a believer in Jesus, you become an heir of God,[3] or as I like to think of it, a daughter of the King. We get to walk through life with confidence that our help comes from the maker of heaven and earth.[4] And our heavenly Father, the One who promises to help us will whisper to you just like He did to me.

Before I heard that whisper in Glencoe, I had underestimated the mightiness of God and His love for me. When I was told that God is with me when I was young, the words fell flat. They didn't comfort me or guide me, not because they were the wrong words but because I simply had not experienced either the majesty of God or felt His powerful, personal love. Thanks to the whisper I heard in that quiet moment, I received both truths and my understanding changed.

God is always whispering to us. That's what good Fathers do, because they want their children close, so they can be with them, so they can teach them, and so they can help them. God is chasing us with His love, offering us countless moments of reconciliation. It's up to us to respond—to slow down, notice His whispers, feel His love, and turn toward Him.

A whisper from God won't always make sense right away, and maybe at first you won't know what you feel. But when you get quiet enough to hear Him, you know that something has happened and that you're different. You will know the delight of being seen, heard, and understood at a soul-deep level. When you feel this stirring in your soul, let the mystery and delight captivate your attention. Let it guide you back to the One calling your name.

Perfect days still have imperfect conditions. Princesses still have imperfect stories. Things don't always look the way we expect—but as children who wear an invisible crown, we can be confident that there's always more to the story.

The world will try to make you forget who you are, encouraging sky-high expectations and your own desire for control or safety or significance. It's part of the enemy's tactic—to make us forget who we are as children of God. It is in the quiet that you will hear His whispers and remember the truth of who you are and where you belong. It's when you seek the quiet and choose to listen for that whisper that you will remember you are a child of the King, held close to His heart and in His arms.[5] It's then you will hear and know, *I see you. I'm with you. I love you.*

CHAPTER 2

Discovering Delight in Dark Places

I was blessed with 20/20 vision. However, I was blind for a decade of my adult life. I don't mean literally, but spiritually. My eyes worked, but my heart didn't. I stayed so busy that it was easy to avoid this gap in my life, but the truth is that I couldn't see who I really was—or who God is. The church told me I was one of God's children, but I couldn't see how that mattered in my life. I actually felt like a nobody, not a child of God.

I hadn't always felt that way, though. Jesus and I were best of friends when I was a little girl. I read my Bible, attended prayer meetings, and ticked all the boxes to be a good girl. I brought my innocent faith into all areas of my life, and I had confidence that He was always with me. I knew that, even when things were bad, He was there. Until the day I looked for Him and couldn't find Him.

It was the first time in my life I had truly felt abandoned. And it was one time I needed Him the most. I woke up naked, with a strange man on top of me, being choked, almost-to-death. I had no idea how I got there, how to get away, or where God was in my time of need.

Throughout my childhood, I'd occasionally think God wasn't listening. I had a list of unanswered prayers—for my parents' marriage to improve, for weight loss, for financial windfall—but in those scenarios the unanswered prayer didn't feel like the reflection of an unloving God.

This time was different.

I looked, and looked, and looked, and found no trace of Him.

Eventually I learned He *had* been there the whole time. It took ten years—and better vision—to see the full picture and understand what had happened. Like searching for a word that doesn't exist, the harder I looked, the further away from the truth I got.

For ten years I blocked out the memory of my assault. It wasn't the trauma itself that haunted me, but the separation from the God who I thought was my friend. In my mind my heavenly Father went from being a friend who loved and protected me, never leaving my side, to being a distant ruler who didn't care enough to save me when I needed Him most. I repackaged Him through this lens and turned off my heart. No matter how I thought about what had happened, I couldn't see Him there. Surely, He had not been there the night I fought for my life.

I was twenty-six years old. Targeted, drugged, taken, and assaulted. They later found me weeping and slumped over in a sand dune, like a worthless piece of trash tossed away. I couldn't tell those who found me what happened or even speak my name.

Following the incident, I went dark on God. My Bible collected dust, and my church attendance became sporadic. I wasn't angry at God; I just felt numb and disconnected. When I couldn't explain where He was when I was in my worst pain, I stopped trying.

As I navigated my post-traumatic stress, I suppressed all memories of that night and built emotional walls of protection. I made a decision that I would not be a victim of what that man had done to me, and I started pouring my energy into rebuilding my life and mental health. I was grateful to be alive.

Years passed. My life changed. I got married and started a family. I was happier than I ever imagined possible. And yet something deep in me would surface from time to time, something so dark and unsettling, so fear-inducing that it would drive me to overcompensate to dangerous levels in my life. I coped by working long hours, setting higher goals, and by obsessively striving after whatever achievement was my priority.

The exhaustion of chasing a moving finishing line left me feeling more and more empty. Many areas of my life were going well, but the more I ticked off the boxes of success, the less loved—and worthy of love—I felt. I was still the girl who was too weak to fight off her attacker. I was still the girl whose dignity was disposable for the carnal whims of a strange and faceless man.

The striving protected me. But the cost for the temporary strength it gave me was a life of never-enough-ness, high-anxiety, and record levels of performance-induced stress. I started cracking, and the undoing drove me even more desperately toward the god of performance I worshipped.

It was then that my mother-in-law, a licensed Christian therapist, suggested that I work with someone trained in Eye Movement Desensitization and Reprocessing (EMDR), psychotherapy proven to ease distress from deeply rooted traumatic memories. Reluctantly, I agreed it was worth a shot, and I began a twelve-week therapy program.

I wasn't sure what we would uncover, but I was sure that I needed to find the exit ramp from the endless highway of proving myself and trying to earn love.

For twelve weeks I drove across town to meet my therapist, Haley. Each time, I gripped my travel coffee mug tight and sat upright in her teal suede chair with my feet kicked out, trying to look comfortable but feeling too anxious to relax. While I was eager to uncover whatever was keeping me stuck, antici-pating the results common in EMDR therapy left me terrified of facing the demons hidden in my memory.

My experience was exactly as my mother-in-law predicted: transformational. I walked away from every session with clar-ity, healing, and peace, and I began recommending EMDR therapy to practically everyone I knew. Then, one day during a session with Haley, the heavens opened.

And by that, I mean God unfroze a blacked-out memory, brought it to full-color, and helped me see what had *actually* happened, not what I *thought* had happened.

I would have never imagined that it would take a decade and a coffee mug of courage to look at my most terrifying moment with real insight. After all that time, I didn't expect God would pull back the curtains of darkness and show me the light that I'd never seen before. But that is exactly what happened in my therapist's office that afternoon—and what I learned was illuminating.

It turns out God had turned the day of my death into the day of my deliverance. The day that I had worked to forget is now the day of my life I want to always remember.

In that moment, I encountered the heart of God and felt closer to Him than I had ever before in my entire life. I began to think that maybe I was His dear child after all. I saw the Jesus who overturns tables out of righteous anger and the God who strikes down evil. I experienced the God who will move the heavens on my behalf, with the wild and wonderful wrath only possible of a Father protecting the dignity, righteousness, and life of His daughter.

As I sat across from Haley, the memories my brain had erased to guard me from the trauma flooded back into my mind with full force.

The night God rescued me started as a perfect day. I was on a family vacation and the resort was filled with life and positive energy. That evening my sun-kissed skin felt like it was glowing as I danced with my cousins to beach music under palm trees. I felt safe, loved, and alive.

And then I woke up somewhere else. I did not know how I got there, and I still don't. The room was dark and musty. I was pinned down, but that didn't matter because my body couldn't move on its own accord, anyway. A strange, muscular man hovered over me, pressing on my body and putting insane pressure on my throat. He had a wired pattern tattoo across his low abdomen and as it moved I felt like chains were being wrapped around my body.

I opened my mouth to scream, but nothing came out. I was screaming for my life, but no sound emerged. I couldn't understand why I was silenced, why I couldn't move, or where my voice had gone. I didn't know where I was. I didn't understand the pain I felt. I didn't even know my name.

But the one thing I knew is that I *needed* to scream. If I didn't scream, I would surely die. But the cries would not emerge.

Something constricted my throat. The pressure came from hands I could not see, from the body that pinned me down so painfully. None of that mattered. The pain he was inflicting with the rest of his body was unnoticeable compared to the strangulation of his hands around my neck. All I felt was darkness and my life slipping away.

Silently, I screamed. I could feel the echo of silence reverberate around me, taunting me into submission. And as my subconscious wrestled between defeat and the reality of what was happening, my heart uttered a prayer. My lips widened with silent pleas and my eyes closed as my prayer emerged: *"Lord, if you give me a voice, I will use it."*

The rapist continued his assault. He had put me under a drug-induced stupor, and it paralyzed my body. His hands expertly squeezed my throat as effortlessly as if my body were Jell-O. He had put my body into his submission, and he choked my voice and breath into silence too.

Then the silence broke.

Shrieks bounced from the walls surrounding me. I wasn't screaming. I was trying to, but I had no air with which to form words. I knew the screams weren't mine, but I couldn't place where they came from. The echoes of their cry didn't match the rhythm of my silent throat, but they were in the same room I was. But it was just me and him in that room.

The cries were undeniable. I knew what I heard wasn't *human*. The voices weren't mine, but they were there *for* me.[6] They interceded for me, on a heavenly decree, until my voice was given life again. The confusion of their shouts provoked a dramatic change in the dingy atmosphere of the room.

As I heard the screams move through the room, confusion ensued. The angels all around me shouted louder and louder. The pressure increased upon my throat and at the precipice of blackout, a *miracle* happened. I yelled for help.

My limp body regained life, not with movement, but with one word. *Help.* I could finally cry out. Paired with the screams of the angels surrounding me, it was loud enough to alarm my assailant into a state of distraction.

The drug intended to silence me lost its power. In a momentary break from the paralysis and amnesia, the impossible became possible.

After that, I don't know what happened, or how help arrived, but it did. Sometime later I was found, in tears, curled up in a dune. Tossed into the sea of people on holiday, I was just another stranger who simply appeared to have lost control. I was scooped up by resort bouncers and treated like a drunk separated from their pack. They wrote me off as irresponsible and as an irritation. No one knew it wasn't alcohol incapacitating me, but the ketamine that filled my veins against my wishes.

Finally, a stranger put a cell phone against my ear. I could hear words, but I muttered animal noises in response. I wasn't capable of words or of speaking. The amnesia reigned heavy in my brain and I didn't know where I was, who I was, or what had happened. I just needed to be safe.

And eventually the people I loved found me. It was all that mattered.

$$\sim$$

In Haley's office the memory of that night came alive. I felt the full intensity of the strangulation as if I were losing my breath again in that moment. Tears poured from my eyes and my body convulsed in sobs. I knew I was safe sitting with my trusted counselor, and I knew the memory wasn't current—but the trauma that had been lodged in my body came to life and confirmed the narrative that had unfolded in my mind.

Holding my throat with panic, I lost my voice. I gasped. My throat, which had been lined with lacerations after the attack, ached again. It felt like acid had filled my throat. My heart raced into full flight mode and I looked across the room at Haley and shook. She locked eyes with me, filled with compassion, and guided me through this unexpected redemption.

God had answered my plea. He had plucked me from the pit. He had rescued me from the dark. I had cried out to the Lord, and He *had* heard my cry. He more than heard my cry; He dispatched angels to arrange my release. He broke the chains of a drug that should have kept me paralyzed and gave my vocal cords power over the enormous hands lodged around my throat.

God had not watched from afar and turned His back on me, as I had once thought. He was more than there; He was *with* me. Next to me. Breathing into me. He brought my screams to life, joining them with those of the angels, and ultimately creating the chaos that led to my rescue.

I don't remember what my counselor said or how long we talked after that, but I know we sat in that office together in awe and with chills running down our limbs. The waterfall of tears continued, but the texture changed. They were no longer a downpour of distress but shouts of reverence. And together, in that sacred space, we worshipped. We marveled at the delight God has for His children and at the lengths He will take to keep them safe.

That mindset of awe and worship didn't last, though. I felt like a tsunami of love had swallowed me up, but it seemed too good to be true. In fact, it terrified me. My mind swirled, desperate to explain away the clarity I had in my fresh memory. Cynicism showed up quickly, almost instantaneously, chiding me for being so childish in my faith to think that God would open the heavens for me and reminding me that no one really *knows* if angels exist.

"Impossible," I thought. "This story can't possibly be true."

Before I could even finish my cynical thought, my mind was jarred with the memory of a post I had made to my social media just an hour prior. *"What is impossible for man is possible with God,⁷"* I had quickly typed before hitting the button to publish it. It's a Bible verse I had shared, rather unwillingly. Those words had sort of chased me around that morning, in a variety of ways, and so unusually so that it somewhat bothered me. It had appeared in an email from a friend. I noticed it in a devotional. It was on my mind all morning and I couldn't shake it from my brain. Fatigue was making me irritated, and I was dreading my appointment with Haley.

With some annoyance, I remember whispering to God as I drove to Haley's office, "God, I get it, I get it. Anything is possible with You. Okay, let's let this verse go, all right?"

Then, just minutes before my meeting with Hayley, I felt prompted to post the verse on social media. I *didn't* want to. I wasn't in the habit of posting Bible verses publicly. It felt awkward. In the waiting room I picked up my phone, opened my app, starting posting, then swiped up and threw my phone into my purse, discounting the urge. Twice. Then Hayley opened her door, and it relieved me. But instead of welcoming me in, she told me she needed a few more minutes. Her tardiness was unusual and while I waited, for the third time, I dug my phone out from under the mess of diapers, wipes, crumbs, and coins that make their home in my purse and quickly retyped the verse. I felt peace when I hit "publish," and heard an almost audible whisper from the Lord saying, "Well done, Daughter. That was for somebody to hear later today." A moment later Haley was ready for me.

I would have never guessed that the verse I posted was actually for me, but as I was re-learning, God is in both the tiniest of details and grandest of gestures as He does everything necessary to show us His love.

I wanted to discount the truth of what happened. Those shrieks that saved me couldn't have been angel voices. This had happened in 2009, not 79AD or in the Old Testament. That kind of thing doesn't happen anymore. It was impossible.

What is impossible for man is possible with God.

Surely, I hadn't been paralyzed, gasping for breath, and then suddenly able to yell for help after whispering a dying prayer of desperation. That would be a miracle, and inexplicable. That would have been impossible.

What is impossible for man is possible with God.

Those supernatural screams that caused the chaos that made my rescue possible are inexplicable. My assailant had seemed prepared and experienced, not easily shaken. If it weren't for that holy chaos, I would not have escaped and ended up in the sand at the feet of strangers who served as the doorway to safety. That would have been impossible.

What is impossible for man is possible with God.

As the words of that verse ran through my mind, over and over, the last bit of cynicism I was holding onto slipped away. I couldn't deny that God had been there. He had been there, with me, in the worst moment of my life. And not just there, but close enough to hear my wordless whisper, my cry for salvation, my silent groanings. And when He answered my prayer, He opened the heavens and sent an army of angels to do it. God was there—and He rescued me.

What is impossible for man is possible with God.

Even now as I contemplate this, the love I feel seems, well, impossible. How could the God of the universe care so profoundly for me He would part the heavens and send an army after me? How could it be that those tears unseen, those cries unheard, those horrors done in the dark weren't unnoticed but made the Lord of the Heavens quiver in anger and righteousness? I don't know how it's possible, but I know it's true. I know God saw me isolated, assaulted, and lost, and He came after me. He rescued me, the way a shepherd does when he leaves his ninety-nine to find the one that's lost.[8]

It's God's impossible love for us that makes *everything* possible. We should never underestimate His incomprehensible desire to save us, to be close to us, and to protect us. He moves mountains. He opens the heavens. He sends His son to earth to die for our sins. There is nothing He will not do to let us know how loved we are.

In that moment of absolute darkness, the moment in my life that I felt most distant from God, I had actually been closer to Him than ever before. Understanding this changed everything for me. It made me look more closely at the other areas in my heart that felt so wounded. And I discovered that there's always more to the story than I can see or feel.

God *hadn't* been looking the other way. No, He had been weeping and singing songs of deliverance over me. He had orchestrated a mighty rescue worthy of any closing scene of an epic movie. Because that's what good fathers do when their beloved child is in need—they move heaven and earth with their love to save the creation they so deeply love.

The story you *think* you have lived to this point might not be the complete story. The role you've believed God has played in your pain might not be what you think it is. I don't know your story, but here's what I know about God: He loves you, and He will not leave you. God has not abandoned you. What I was blind to see but know for certain now is that abandoning you, or me, is simply not in His nature.[9]

He is the God who does the unexpected. He turns the world upside down. He is the God who will take your darkest moment and transform it into the most intimate moment of delight and love you will ever experience. And best of all, neither height nor depth, nor anything that has, can, or will happen in your life story can ever keep you from the love of God.[10] Quite the contrary, the delight we can feel despite the darkness gives us a deeper ability to see the lovingkindness of God.

The Author is not done with our stories, and not all stories are told the same. For some, we get a linear, clear picture. For others, we catch bits and pieces. Sometimes, like in the story I shared, we have our mysteries made known to us. But sometimes, we never have eyes to see where God was and where He is taking us.

So, while we cannot be certain of the narrative style of our lives, we can be sure of one thing. God has a better story for our lives than we could ever even imagine. We don't need to obsess or have to control the details, because God tells us explicitly in the Bible that He loves us[11] and He is for us. And if God is for us, who can be against us?[12] As daughters of the King, we know we will have trials and tribulation in this world,[13] but that ultimately, our King will work all things together for our good.[14] We know how our story will end. It will be good.

I don't know your story, but I do know that you and I share what matters the most: the love of God. From the moment He formed you in your mother's womb until the last breath you take, your Creator sees you, knows you, and loves you.

CHAPTER 3

Discovering Delight in Being Seen

I t started with a comment from a friend. We were ten years old, hanging out at our neighborhood pool. I was in my Speedo one-piece, and she and her gorgeous twin sister wore sparkly bikinis that I would never have been allowed to wear. Every boy at Lake of the Woods had a crush on those twins, meanwhile I was happy simply to be friends with them and earn cool points by association.

She didn't mean to hurt me. But her words stung my heart in a way that burned deeply into my identity for over a decade later. "Your brother is *so* hot," she started. Continuing, she added, "You look nothing like him. Are you *sure* you have the same parents?"

Everyone laughed. I waited desperately for the lifeguard's whistle to blow, allowing me to escape underwater into the pool. I remember diving in, trying to run away from the shame. Everyone wanted to be seen with my brother. And, if according to her words, I truly was nothing like him, that meant that I wasn't worth being seen.

It embarrassed me. I felt deep shame in how I looked and how God made me.

I couldn't point to the exact problem, either. My body was athletic, strong and lean for a little girl, and I was well-liked for being an excellent swimmer. But being liked for what I could do felt very different from being liked for who I was or how I looked.

During high school and college, I convinced myself that I was forgettable. Sure, my teammates, classmates, and friends knew who I was, but in general? I believed I looked so average that people wouldn't remember me. I was certain that the people I passed in the halls daily looked through me, that I merely blended in with the masses.

Perhaps you are like me. I believed I had value for what I could do, not necessarily for who I was. I desperately craved significance, but how could I matter if I was average, unseen, or forgettable?

Little by little, though, God started rewiring my understanding of myself, starting with showing me how much I mattered to Him. I couldn't help noticing little things that made me smile—like seeing bunnies when I was out walking or an unusual amount of super pink sunsets, my favorite—began appearing more often. I had convinced myself that God was too busy for me, but the way I started seeing Him show up in my daily life was undeniable. He was going out of His way to bring me delight in the everyday, simply because He not just noticed me, but He loved me. Then He shook things up even more.

When I was in high school, I had been praying for money. My wealthier friends were all able to attend a Christian retreat over spring break, but the $500 price tag was out of the question for my family. A mentor had offered me a partial scholarship, but I still needed to come up with $100 for food costs. My parents were living paycheck to paycheck, I couldn't get any extra lifeguarding hours because of my already busy schedule, and I was too embarrassed to ask any of my friends for help. The $100 might as well have been $1,000 for me. It just was not possible.

Shortly before spring break, I was in Philadelphia for a school function. On our last night there, as I crossed the street with a group of students, I noticed a brown paper bag in the middle of the street. It was dark and rainy, and we were in an unfamiliar neighborhood. Normally, I would have never even kicked this bag, let alone touched it. But that night the rain had soaked the bag, tearing it ever so slightly and making the brownness thin out a bit. Through the rain-soaked bag I saw the faintest hint of green paper, enough that my curiosity made me bend down to investigate.

What I picked up was a sopping wet $100 bill.

I looked around to find the owner, but only saw my classmates and our coach. A peace swept over me like I had never experienced—and it came with a whisper to my soul that I couldn't shake. The whisper wasn't audible, but it was clear in my heart as it said: *Never doubt that I can't make money fall from the sky for you, dear daughter. I see you. I hear you. You matter.*

Driving home in the van felt surreal. Everyone marveled at my good luck, but I knew it was more than luck. I knew God saw me. And I knew my faith in God's provision in my life would never look the same. God can make money fall from the sky.

I felt grateful and amazed, but also a little confused. Let's be honest—being this loved by the God of the universe, the God who created everything, makes little sense. How could He have time for us? Or even notice us and care for us?

But He does, and He does so in ways so intricately intimate and attentive that our human minds can't comprehend or fathom.[15] He does because we aren't just a somebody to Him—we are His daughters, His heirs, His little princesses.[16]

Money continued to be a problem for my family as I grew up. The atmosphere of financial fear was ever present. Most of the time we lived paycheck to paycheck; we scrimped to get by, and it always felt like it would never be enough. I never felt secure and the future always felt uncertain.

This prepared me well for the entrepreneurial world. I learned how to be okay with risk and uncertainty.

As I entered the business world years later, little wins piled up. My experience living with risk and uncertainty gave me enough courage to keep moving forward in my chosen field. One of the first revenue wins that gave me hope was a mobile app I created. It was a half-marathon training app that was immediately successful, a success that has lasted for years. Every month, for years, I received financial manna from heaven—direct from Apple Incorporated into my little business checking account.

Hoping to replicate that initial app's success, I invested in creating other apps for people looking for fitness motivation. A few of the apps sold, but most didn't. One app was my favorite, Ab Randomizer, and it worked like an exercise slot machine. With the push of a button, you would get a custom-designed workout to help keep your life in the gym interesting and effective. Unfortunately, the Ab Randomizer stayed fitness' best-kept secret, averaging between two and three downloads per day. At ninety-nine cents per download, that means I netted a measly profit of about $1.50 per day. It was a bummer.

Then, one Tuesday at work I opened up my email as normal. I checked my app download stats, as was my routine, but when I opened my daily email from Apple, the numbers were not what I expected.

Sure, my golden goose half-marathon app did what it always did—it was manna, and consistent manna. The shock came from the Ab Randomizer. Instead of seeing one or even two dollars on its report, the number said $900. I thought it was a typo until I saw a spike in the corresponding download report graph. It was truly an incredible increase of downloads for an app that was otherwise dead.

Again, God can drop money from the sky. And He can do it on any day, in any way that He likes. Nothing is beyond Him.

I triple checked my numbers, contacted my support team, and did everything to make sure that my eyes were reading the report correctly. And sure enough, something had tripped the app algorithm and Ab Randomizer had been downloaded in one day over 1,500 times.

Perhaps even more important to add to this story happened the next day. I opened my email report, eager to see a duplication of the day prior, but it wasn't the same. The Ab Randomizer went right back to three downloads and two dollars of income.

Once again, I felt God smile toward me. He got my attention and stretched my faith through unexpected money. Money that felt like it had literally come from the sky. And in my heart, I heard him say, *Yes, I'm here. Yes, I see you. Yes, I can drop money from Heaven for you. Daughter, you are secure. The circumstances in front of you might not feel secure, but in me you are always secure.*

He got my attention that day. It wasn't the financial windfall that so moved me, but the emotional security that gave me spiritual provision that I didn't even know I needed. And it stretched my faith, forcing my belief to stretch beyond what I thought was possible or reasonable. I had been pulling away from Him and seeking meaning in my success and efforts.

But that day I saw and felt just how real God was—and remembered both how much He cared about me and how much I needed Him. I also found security in not being reliant on my self-sufficiency. It humbled me because there was nothing I did to earn that extra $898 that day. He just dropped it into my bank account, a divinely orchestrated fluke of the algorithm that did just the right job to get my attention.

God is like that. He does those things and more. He wants our attention, for with our attention comes our affection. The most distinguishing feature of Christianity versus any other religion is that Christianity is grounded on the fundamental belief that God is a relational God. Like any relationship, it's two-sided and interactive.

Have you ever been in a one-sided relationship? You know, one where you made all the effort and received a minimal response in return? You might have called it a relationship, but it really wasn't. We define a relationship as a state of being connected and interactive.

I grew up in the church, so conversation about having a "relationship with God" was common language. My parents and Sunday School teachers taught me to have a relationship with God by reading my Bible, going to church, and talking to God. It made sense. I understood my part of being in a relationship.

Never, though, did I consider the relationship from the other perspective. I mean, I had learned that God's part of the relationship was to not send me to hell. I understood He sacrificed His only Son for my sins, and that was the greatest gift anyone could ever ask for in a relationship. As far as I was concerned, God had completed His part of being in relationship with me by writing my name in the book of life that gives access to Heaven and occasionally answering some of my prayers.

My small view of God inhibited my ability to see His hand and take part in my relationship with Him. I had cheapened it, unintentionally. I just never thought about Him being an active and caring participant in my life. My view of God being distant, too big for me, and cold had limited my ability to see Him for who He really is.

God is an active participant in our lives. It's who He is; He is a relational God.[17] He cares about the things in our lives. He cares about what makes you smile and what makes you sad.

God wants good things for you. He can't help Himself, it's in His nature.[18]

I know I can't resist buying good things for my kids, particularly overpriced toys, when they're not with me. When I see something that I know will just absolutely delight my children, like a Kinder Surprise, a Paw Patrol lollipop, or a Disney Princess sticker book, I buy it. Even if the gift wasn't in my budget or isn't something they actually need, it's worth the deep internal satisfaction I get, thinking about the joyful surprise they have awaiting them.

That's what a parent does. And God is not just any parent; He's the perfect parent. It is who He is—He is good;[19] He is kind;[20] He is faithful;[21] He is intricately engaged in the details of our lives.[22]

I am convinced that God smiles at the things that make me smile. Just like when I was a child, certain sunsets, the ones that are a palette of pink swirls, feel like they are just for me. Knowing that I have always had a love for bunnies, the inordinate number of little rabbits that I see every day is not short of extraordinary. He moves in and around my day in a way that catches my eye and makes me smile.

That smile is reserved for special moments. It's how you smile when a friend unexpectedly brings you your favorite Starbucks drink to your office. Or when you snag a front-row parking spot at Walmart on a Saturday morning. It's the smile we give when things are going our way and life just feels good.

Before you can comprehend that God sees you, you first have to experience being seen—for who you really are, not for what you do—by a human. This sounds basic and obvious, but most of us live such busy, achievement-focused lives that we connect being seen with what we do. But being seen for what you do isn't very impressive; in fact, it's rather dull and expected. In a world that celebrates attention and fame, it's easy to understand how we got it wrong and believed the same. If we only feel seen for what we do—for how we look, what we achieve, or who we know—then we aren't really seen for who we are at our core.

It is what is on the inside that matters the most. God looks at the heart.[23] Truth be told, most people likely feel most connected to and influenced by people because of who they *were on the inside*, not the outside. Still, being more concerned with outward things is an easy trap to fall into without even realizing how deep in you really are. I know I didn't see it coming myself.

Then, when I was in my thirties, I met my therapist, Denise.

Before I met Denise, countless people saw me for me. I didn't know it, though. As I mentioned earlier, I felt invisible and forgettable. Determined to stand out, I became distracted by performing and achieving, so I misinterpreted the acceptance and love that were offered freely. The more I excelled, the more well-loved I felt, and so I developed a deep need for status, success, and being impressive. I wanted to stand out; I wanted to be seen.

I'll never forget the first ten minutes of my first therapy appointment. Denise sat across from me silently. She was waiting for me to finish. She had asked me who I was, and I spent quite a while listing out the things I did. After allowing silence to fill the room for a moment, she said: "I didn't ask you what you do. I asked you who you are."

Ouch.

It confused me. She went deeper, though, and without hesitation. "I am not impressed by what you do," she whispered. "I am eager to learn who you are—that's what matters. I work with many people who do a lot of impressive things, but you need to know that those things don't even stir me."

That was it. Denise called me out in those first few minutes of our meeting. She was the first person who challenged me to see myself differently. I had never thought that way before. My entire life had been an effort to do things well enough that I would be seen or noticed.

Before we were formed, God knew us.[24] He had planned for us and waited for the perfect timing to give us breath.[25] He loved us before we even existed and could do anything—because He loves us for who He made us to be, not what we do. He gave you an assignment,[26] but He won't force you into showing up for it. Your free will is a gift; you can do with your life as you choose. And whatever you choose God's love for you remains the same. He detaches His love for us from how we show up for our assignment.[27] Nothing we can do will make Him love us more, and nothing we can do will make Him love us less.[28]

There's nothing you can do to make God love you anymore than He already does. Likewise, there is nothing you can do to make Him love you any less. When we are faithful to the assignment divinely placed in us, we don't earn more love but what we do experience is more peace.[29]

These truths came to life for me, instilling such peace in my heart, as I continued to meet with Denise and learn from her how valued I am simply for who I am. When we talked, I knew she wouldn't care what I had accomplished each week, how much revenue my business had brought in, or how brilliant my writing had been. She separated my value from those things, and she leaned in to listen closer to my heart, to the part of me that makes me really me.

Do you have a Denise in your life, someone who leans into you? I hope you do, but if you haven't found that person yet, I want you to hear the same truths she has shown me. You matter. You are not invisible or easily forgotten. The things you might think define you—where you came from, who you know, or what you've accomplished—don't. Separate from all of those things, you are a daughter of the King, a child of God, and He sees you as tremendously important.

My parents raised me to have a relationship with God. I knew Jesus loved me. I memorized Bible verses. I understood that the Lord knew us by name, counted our hairs, and made each of us special. But, for a little girl who didn't believe that anyone actually wanted to be around her for who she was instead of for what she did, I could have never comprehended that He would show me, over and over throughout my life, how intimately He sees and knows me, how deeply He longs to be in relationship with me.

But I see now that it's true. That's what He's saying. To me, and to you. Sister, He doesn't just see you; He is reaching into your everyday life in ways designed specially to touch your heart. Because your heart—not your resume or your skills or your successes or even your failures—is what He cares about most of all. Under all of those things, He sees the real you. And He wants to be in a real, two-sided, reciprocal relationship with you—the kind where you finally know that He sees you and that you are enough.

CHAPTER 4

Discovering Delight Through Disappointment

The critical voice is a thief.

You know that voice. It's the one that fills you with self-doubt and shame. It's the one that says you're behind, not capable or stuck. It's the one that criticizes you, that puts down, and that pressures you to feel you need to do more. It's the voice that leads to feeling constantly disappointed.

It steals life. It crushes hope. It robs us of goodness and love.

Sometimes it sneaks in with a whisper, and other times it storms in with a yell. It will do whatever it takes to capture your attention. And when it does, its suggestions and criticisms feel very real and very true.

Criticism doesn't work for your benefit. Being critical doesn't add joy. It doesn't get better results. It doesn't bring more success. It doesn't keep things running. It just steals. Every single time. The critical voice is a thief, and always a thief.

My mind used to be a very loud place. It echoed an un-ending refrain of not-enough-ness and self-criticism. I lived in a state of disappointment. On the outside, I looked happy, but inside, a war was raging. I was fighting for my place in the world. I was desperate to be worthy of love.

It didn't matter what I did; I always felt like I could have done better. I believed that an "A" on a paper could have been an "A+", a pay raise could have been a larger increase, and an achievement only set me up to focus on the next level of achievement. I never felt good enough and always felt like I could do more or do better.

I was constantly disappointed in myself or how things were working out for me.

Disappointment is an all-too-familiar friend for many of us. It looks different, and sometime sneaks in unsuspectingly, but ultimately it always brings the same whisper: *you are not enough*.

On the surface, disappointment is a mismatch between re-ality and expectations—and the criticism that can sneak in creates a wider chasm between the two worlds. But, if we can see how delight shows up in disappointment, we can see some-thing very different.

In order to change our relationship with disappointment, we have to acknowledge our default setting with it first. Un-monitored disappointment can go deep into the bones. It be-comes not just about something that happened, but about us, and our worthiness as humans. We take simple rejections and over-personalize them to mean something more than what they do.

I get rejected for a gig. *Disappointment sets in.*

Someone says something negative about me and I feel rejected. *Disappointment sets in.*

What I see in the mirror chips away at my self-esteem. *Disappointment sets in.*

I wish I was further along in my career than I am. *Disappointment sets in.*

I look at someone else's Instagram life and think they're happier and luckier than me. *Disappointment sets in.*

The voice of disappointment is the voice of discontentment. It is the unsettled feeling we get when we feel jealousy that someone else's life *appears* to be going *better* than ours. For me, it's the self-criticism over my failings, my weaknesses, my awkwardness, my weight, my whatever-I-can-think-of that I just don't like about myself.

Perhaps you have lived with a critical voice in your life too?

It's the voice that doesn't let you relax. The one that tells you that enough is never enough. The one that compares your behind-the-scenes life to the filtered highlight reels that others curate on social media.

It took me almost destroying myself—working myself into exhaustion and living with a burden of unshakeable inadequacy—before I realized that the critical spirit in my life was killing me.

The thief comes only to kill and destroy,[30] and that's exactly what criticism does.

Criticism has a best friend. Its name is disappointment.

The two of them go hand in hand. Typically, where one goes, there too you will find the other. I never considered myself someone burdened by the voice of criticism. But *disappointment,* now that was something I never seemed able to shake.

Even as a kid, I feared my mom's disappointment more than her anger. After all, anger passes. It simply highlights something we have done wrong, but disappointment is different. It digs in its heels into our wounded place—our identity. It makes us believe that there is something wrong with who we are.

As a child, I was constantly disappointed in myself. Though my parents weren't overly critical of me, I picked up the spirit of disappointment from them. Like most hard-working families that struggled with money, life often felt disappointing. Disappointment is an emotion many of us learn from an early age, and it's one we must learn to manage our entire lives. If we don't learn how to manage it, we can get stuck in those earliest disappointments.

I can still remember the day I was devastated by disappointment—when I realized my dreams of Olympic glory were unattainable. The disappointment ravished my soul. I was in boarding school and it was 1999. The 2000 Olympics were on the horizon, but I was nowhere near them or even talks of Sydney. I was lying on a bunk bed in Chatham, middle-of-nowhere, Virginia, crying and filled with shame. I thought my future and purpose had gotten a downgrade. Someone had just broken my national record, wiping my name from the swimming history books, and I was losing more frequently than I was winning. I felt like a nobody.

I had gone from being ranked first in the world to fighting for name recognition within state rankings. In my mind, my life's purpose was to swim in the Olympics. This was *the* way to matter—and anything other than this was a second-best option, the one for the loser I didn't want to be.

The path that once had felt so obvious became rocky, and then non-existent. I floated in a nebulous world where I felt like a fraud, didn't have hope for my future, but kept doing what I was doing, feigning belief that my efforts would make a difference.

What I remember most from that time is the loneliness I felt. It wasn't because I didn't have friends, or teammates, or mentors and coaches. I felt lonely because I felt less than. It embarrassed me. What do you do when you have only one dream and that dream is dead?

I was disappointed in myself.

Disappointment, when it sinks into our bones, disconnects us. It un-tethers us from our place in our community and family, distancing us with shame and unworthiness. It is isolating.

The failure in my athletic endeavors stung deeper with each dive I took into the pool. I couldn't understand why other people weren't struggling the way I was. The harder I worked, the slower I swam. I increased the pressure I put on myself, and the more I did, the more my performance and happiness decreased.

Criticism is like that. It creates pressure and pressure suffocates.

The more pressure I put on myself to swim better, the slower I swam. I swam in shame over who I had become. I was a failure. The envy and comparison I felt overwhelmed me. I was a disappointment to my coaches. I was someone who wasn't able to tap into her full potential. I had coach after coach preach to me about my potential—and about how I could make a splash at an international level—if I could just stop messing up and stop getting in my own way.

Increased pressure created increased expectations, which combusted into increased disappointment. My heart ached. The more disappointing I felt, the more unlovable I became. I was embarrassed of myself and I pushed others away.

Technically, I had a successful swimming career. I earned a full scholarship—a free education. I earned recognition within the collegiate ranks with a 4x All-American All-Academic status, and I competed in both national and international championships. But it all still felt like a joke. I didn't dare share with anyone how I really felt about myself, because on paper I was achieving things that *should* have filled me with gratitude. I didn't want to appear ungrateful, so I let the disappointment drive a divide between me and everyone else.

I felt like I had let God down. I thought He was going to use me in this world because of my swimming. And I had let the ball drop. He gave me talent, and I botched it. I couldn't see beyond the plan I created for myself, and when I couldn't live out the plan, I was sure that God was disappointed in me too.

The critical voice is cunning. It knows how to weave in and out of your thoughts and memories, anchoring stains of shame at every chance presented. For me, just looking at an old picture of myself, if I am not on guard for the critical voice, can make me spiral.

We are told to be on guard, for the enemy prowls like a roaring lion back and forth to devour us.[31] What I didn't realize for a long time was that he was destroying me by suggesting thoughts and dialogue to make me first destroy myself. I lost all faith, which is what the enemy is after. If he can squash our faith, he can render us useless for good in this world.

There is a battle for our faith, and it happens in our thoughts.

Unruly thoughts will sneak into your brain every day. And so, we have to clean out, choose, and manage our thoughts every day. Thought work, or taking our thoughts captive, isn't easy. [32] And it never stops. But the more we do it, the more proficient we will become.

The other day I came across some pictures of my husband and me from our engagement trip to France. He proposed to me in one of my favorite spots in Paris, *les Jardins de Luxembourg*, while we were doing my favorite thing: having a picnic.

Everything about the moment was perfect. In my memory, it feels like a dream. We have a few framed photos around the house commemorating that day—but only the good photos.

Then there are the other photos. You know, the ones that didn't make the cut for the first printing and framing job—unflattering photos with bad lighting or unflattering angles. On the day I believed my dreams had come true, when I felt the *most* beautiful and the *most* loved that I had been my entire life, some photos would say otherwise. Or at least my critical eye would say they do.

My inner critic sees a round face and childish features. It sees fashion choices that could have been better and hair that could have been more elegant. The critic sees poor makeup and a body that could have been five pounds lighter. When I looked at those discarded photos, I heard: *You don't deserve this love. You aren't worthy. You're an embarrassment, and when the people who love you finally discover you're a charity case, they'll leave you.*

Shame practically jumped off the photos and swallowed me up.

The dissonance between the joy and shame I feel about the same day creates conflict in my thoughts, and it feels like standing at a mental crossroad, unsure of which direction is the right one. This intersection used to confuse me, but I've learned to see it as a place to pause, in the same way it would be if I were driving a car before picking a direction to drive.

Those awful photos from my picnic in Paris? They're just bad photos. They mean nothing, nor do they steal from my joy of that day. That seems like obvious reasoning to the outsider, but for me to conclude that requires me to remember that who I am when I stand at the mental crossroads of self-judgment. Each time I have to renew my mind, reminding myself of my identity. I am a child of God. I am a daughter of the King. I am beautifully created.

For years I didn't know that I could think about what I think about. It used to be that when I saw a bad photo—from high school, from college, or even from that day in Paris—I thought that whatever my inner critic said was the truth and the only way I could think about it. But that's simply not true.

We have power over our thoughts,[33] but that doesn't mean that choosing the right thought is easy. It also doesn't mean that it's a one and done decision. Often, deciding which thought to think takes revisiting the right thought repeatedly.

And so, even today, I remind myself repeatedly that a bad picture is just a bad picture—not an accurate reflection of me. In doing that, I preemptively free myself from unfounded and unnecessary disappointment.

Besides feeling disappointment in myself when I let criticism have free rein in my thoughts, I often experience another type of disappointment—the type of disappointment that comes from unmet expectations. I felt this deeply when I found out my second child was going to be a boy, not another girl like I had hoped.

I had been counting down for weeks, waiting for the sonogram to reveal our second child's gender. I was *confident* that it was a girl. So confident that we even had a name picked out for her, even though it was early in the pregnancy. The name Esther Elizabeth felt alive to both my husband and I, and we were certain this was our little Esther.

It was a rainy day when we drove to the doctor's office. My stomach was in knots, eager to confirm my gut instinct. Brandon and I notified the staff to keep the gender from us, as we were having a gender reveal party later that week with family and friends. But while I was lying on the exam table, the nurse squealed, "Oh, I know for sure about this one." She then whispered a quick "sorry" to us and shuffled out of the room. I got an immediate pit in my stomach. Everyone knows boys are easier to identify on sonograms, and her quick assessment ruined the surprise. I played it off but was so distracted when the doctor came in that I barely remember responding to his questions about my geriatric pregnancy risks. I just shook my head, let Brandon speak for me, and tried to keep smiling.

All I could think about was how I was ill-equipped to parent a little boy. My daughter was two, and I could only imagine being a girl mom. I was already thinking about the sister power team Ellie and Esther would be.

We left the office, and I confessed my disappointment to Brandon. On top of being disappointed, I was disappointed that I was disappointed. Yep, I was a hot mess. I started crying, feeling shame and sadness on behalf of my little boy for the feelings that he would never know I ever had. Disappointment manipulates our souls like that—it creeps in and brings with it a wave of shame crashing over our souls. When I feel that, I want to run and hide in my bed with Netflix and an oversized sweatshirt. I shut down and feel numb, disengaging from the world.

We ordered custom cake pops for our gender-reveal party announcement. I knew that I was carrying a boy, but a small part of me still carried a hope that the inside of the cake pops would be pink. But they weren't. Ellie, then two years old, joyfully bit into one as our friends and family gathered around. She looked at the blue cake and smiled ear to ear, not really knowing what "you're getting a little brother" meant but delighted, nonetheless. For a quick moment, I slid into the sweetness of joy with her.

The disappointment—and the subsequent guilt—came back, and I carried it for months. I struggled to pick out a nursery theme for his room, and I couldn't agree with Brandon on a name for him. I asked my closest friends questions about why they loved being a boy mom, desperate to connect with this baby boy. As the weeks passed, my emotions stayed the same, and I couldn't shake my disappointment.

Then, in the blink of an eye, my heart flipped upside down and turned inside out. Five weeks before my due date, I found myself recovering from an emergency C-section, alone in my hospital room and being monitored for seizures. One minute I had been walking through Home Goods, pregnant and unassuming. An hour later I was in a hospital bed and my pregnant stomach was flat. Brandon was with the baby, who we eventually named Baker in the NICU. Once I was alert, he ran to my room to show me a photo of Baker since they would not allow me to be with him for twenty-four hours as both he and I recovered on our respective machines.

I saw his wrinkled body, his platinum blonde head of hair, and his piercing blue eyes—and my heart leapt. I fell in love instantly. The photo showed him attached to what seemed like a dozen machines, but none of that mattered. All I saw was my son, my perfect son, and I wept tears of joy for God's goodness.

I needed *this* little boy. Not the little girl I had imagined. God had this perfect plan all along. And now I cannot imagine my life without my son. I remind myself that even when I feel deep disappointment, I have nothing to fear for God truly has goodness for me however my life unfolds.

I'm reminded that there are things I don't know, and my plans aren't always good ones. It is in these moments I give thanks that God's ways are higher than my ways. His thoughts are higher than mine are.[34] God knows what I need, even when I don't think I need it.

And gosh, y'all. I needed this little boy.

Possibly the most affectionate child on the planet, he covers me with kisses, hugs me in ways that only he can. He is wild— the wild they warn you about with little boys, the jump-off-the roof kind of wild, keeping me on my toes as I try to keep him from hurting himself. I embrace his wildness, though, because it's the kind that comes with unleashed passion of unbridled love and excessive affection. And to think I didn't believe I could parent a little boy.

It is in the unknowns of life that our greatest gifts and experiences come. Baker is possibly the most vibrant gift from God I have ever received and a glorious reminder that God knows what we want and need more than we do. I need that reminder. Like, repeatedly.

Disappointments, whether they are about us or about our circumstances are ultimately a lack of perspective. They reflect our limited viewpoint, and they can hurt deeply. But with God, disappointment changes. He turns it around, He surprises us with what's next, and He has a bigger plan for us than we can even imagine.

I was convinced that God was disappointed in me, from my own personal failures and from the circumstances in my life that didn't go the way I wanted. This belief that I had let God down kept me from fully experiencing the grace of God's love. The truth is that He is not disappointed in me, nor in you. We are his daughters, covered by the blood of His Son. It's time to stop beating ourselves up with self-criticism. Beating yourself up all the time bruises you from the inside out. You can't always see the wounds, but they are there, and they handicap you in a painful, unnecessary way.

Life is guaranteed to come with disappointment, it's part of living in a broken world, and being human. So, since we know disappointments are part of the path, why do we act so surprised and put off by them? Disappointment does not have to discourage us. Instead, it can invite us into emotional boldness and active faith, as we practice praising God for what we know He will turn into something good.[35]

The possibility of disappointment makes life adventurous. It helps us remember that we need God and keeps us craving His presence daily. And with God involved, things become exciting. Like looking forward to reading the next book of your favorite author, you know that what they write next will be good. It's the same with God. He is the ultimate author, and when we give Him the authority to write our story, through the disappointments and all, we can look forward to the next chapter ahead of us with confidence.

CHAPTER 5

Discovering Delight in Sweetness

The land of milk and honey described in Exodus as God's Promised Land for His people has always fascinated me. Because my life was starkly absent of milk and honey—I spent a good portion of my life eliminating those exact things, in fact—so this land I read about in the Old Testament felt like an absolute foreign concept.

For nearly two decades of my life, I didn't drink milk. It was just too caloric when I could choose almond milk instead. Honey? Well, for a girl who lived and died by calorie counting, honey was a decadence reserved for the lucky few with unusually high metabolisms, or for children.

Thankfully, God has done some work on me. In the healing process of my eating disorder, He not only introduced milk and honey back into my diet, but parallelly taught me more than I ever imagined about the land of milk and honey. Most importantly, He showed me how to live in it and possess it for myself.

Honey makes everything taste better. It is sweet nectar with a seemingly impossible consistency; it is perhaps nature's crowning glory. Sadly, I spent about two decades of my life loving honey but lying to myself. Anytime someone offered it—for my toast, for my tea, for my yogurt—I told them I didn't like it. Honey had too much sugar. It was empty calories. It was for other people, not me. I would buy Greek yogurt packets with honey, and then eat around the honey, to avoid calories. I was a prisoner to calorie counting. I wanted out; I wanted freedom but didn't know where to start.

My refusal to allow myself one of my favorite foods was one of many symptoms of my stoic approach to deprivation and it led to a life lived under a cloud of constant self-criticism and pre-emptive disappointment. The disappointment was the worst. Seemingly innocuous, it would creep into my heart as motivation to do better but leave me riddled with shame and sadness. The disappointment irritated my soul, because I simply couldn't make sense of it. Technically, life was going well for me. Yet no matter what I did, the weight of pending disappointment didn't disappear.

On the surface, I had everything I ever wanted. The handsome husband, the dream job, the two beautiful children, the teddy-bear-lookalike dog, and the picture-perfect social media posts. We had the financial means and flexibility for international travel, the robust social life I wanted, and the extended family and church family anyone could ask for. *And yet.*

And yet I felt heaviness with each day. Like I was holding my breath, waiting for the other shoe to drop. Without realizing it, I was walking in blessing and yet refusing to rejoice fully, out of fear of the expected disappointment and letdown to come.

I thought I was wired for it. Expecting things to go wrong was the mindset that dominated my family's home and my parents' childhood homes as well. As a middle-class family we were mostly secure, but there was always financial stress. I never quite felt safe or like things couldn't just fall apart in the blink of an eye or with an unexpected bill. By mere proximity to this belief system, I assumed it was normal to expect things to go wrong.

We can't change our family history, but we can change our family's future. I'm not talking about what has happened, but what is to come. It starts with a simple decision to break patterns of dysfunction or fear. I learned this from my pastor and therapist and, with their help, decided that I could be the change-maker in my family story. I broke the generational voice of disappointment, negativity, criticism, and perfectionism through deep work in therapy, prayer, and thought work around what thoughts I would allow in my mind and which ones I would not. I started by deciding that I didn't agree with the dysfunction passed down to me and determined to escort every fear thought out of my mind every time it snuck back in.

You can do the same with your story and your family. There are things passed down by those who came before you. But just because it got passed to you doesn't mean you have to keep it or hold on to it. You can push it away and exchange it for something better.

God lovingly created you for good works,[36] not perpetual disappointment, not a lifetime waiting for the other shoe to drop, not endless wandering in the desert. No, He created you to live in a land flowing with milk and honey. We don't have full access to this Promised Land on this side of Heaven, but we have the promise that while we are on Earth goodness and unfailing love will pursue us everywhere we go,[37] we will live in joy and peace,[38] and rivers of living water will flow from our hearts.[39]

Honey is a sign of abundance, ease, and prosperity. In ancient times, they considered it a rare luxury and honored gift.[40] Samuel, the Old Testament prophet, refers to it as a sign of good health.[41] And the Bible describes the Promised Land God has set aside for His children as "the land flowing with milk and honey" dozens of times.[42]

The idea that a land of milk and honey is available to me, and not just to the Israelites some three thousand years ago as they fled Egypt, rocked my world. It simply is something I had never considered. It posed such a contrast to my life of restriction and scarcity mindset. I had a busy life, filled with achievement and success by the world's standards, but my heart ached for more. It ached for a life flowing with milk and honey, or goodness and peace.

Paul tells us in the New Testament that knowing the love of Christ gives us access to the fullness of God.[43] This access can fill us to overflowing with peace, joy, strength, and goodness—in other words, milk and honey for our souls. If that's not a promise to hold on to, I don't know what is.

The Bible speaks of the Promised Land with references of flowing abundance. The Promised Land was more than just flowing with good things; it was a place of satisfaction and prosperity.[44]

Sign me up for life in the land of milk and honey. I'm sold.

The honey that I now taste in my life is honey from Heaven, a honey that coats my heart with love, joy, peace, patience, kindness, goodness, faithfulness, gentleness, and self-control.[45] As believers in Christ, we are endowed with this spiritual richness deep within our soul. It is the Holy Spirit, and it gives us power and a peace that surpasses all understanding.[46] This gives us the freedom to live life and have it to the full, the gift that Jesus came to give us,[47] and it's even better than the original Promised Land.

Repeatedly, we are told in the pages of the Bible that He rewards those who seek him[48] and extends favor to those who are faithful.[49] We are told that He will sustain us[50], He will lift us up in honor,[51] and He will fill us with peace.[52] It the deep spiritual richness that we all crave in a world that leaves us endlessly unsatisfied.

For much of my life, though, this wasn't the God I knew. The God I worshiped was caring, but distant. I learned that holiness mattered, not happiness. However, the more I've read God's Word and the more time I've spent in the presence of God, the more I believe it is actually *sacred* to live in such a way that you enjoy everyday life. Our joy—joy that remains constant no matter the circumstances—is one of our most effective testimonies of God's goodness and love to those who don't yet know Him.

It took me a while to get there, though. When I met my husband's family, I was uncomfortable. I was in recovery from an eating disorder, and his family ate dessert with *every* dinner, and sometimes with lunch too. Remember, I never ate dessert. But Brandon's family was healthy and also ate dessert. This was perplexing to me. My mind simply couldn't wrap itself around a healthy family who also consistently ate what I considered unhealthy foods.

Even in recovery from my eating disorder, my relationship with food was complicated, and my behavior around it was unpredictable. To cope, I began lying and using blanket statements and hard boundaries like, "I don't like pizza," and, "I don't like cake." In doing so, I deprived myself of my absolute favorite foods—like honey. It was safer to say I don't like them, than to risk being unable to control my intake of them in public around others. It worked out for me that during this season of my life I was an athlete and a personal trainer, so saying extreme health statements about food was on brand. It was more than just accepted; it was applauded.

So, you can see why a girl like me was so uncomfortable around a family like my husband's. I didn't know how to act around so much food I considered off limits. Fear swallowed me up at the thought of having to create more rules for myself around what foods I didn't like to keep my body weight safe. Anxiety about the lies I was crafting and dieting rules I was worshipping left me exhausted and feeling like a fraud.

I made some rules for myself, and his family worked around my quirkiness and obsession with foods I considered healthy. Marie, Brandon's mom, made allowances for my pickiness and always stocked the house with whatever foods I requested. Her accommodations and flexibility toward me were love incarnate.

Then, one day, Marie made a coconut cake for her husband. We were all gathered as family for a Sunday dinner, and it was the first dessert I couldn't resist. At dozens of dinners and gatherings before this incident, I had said "no thank you" to every dessert. This time, though, I said yes.

My birthday came soon after, and their family tradition was that Marie would cook a dinner of your choice and cake of your choice. For dinner I chose grilled salmon, asparagus, and zucchini, and for the cake, coconut cake. I didn't know then that only Tom and I liked coconut cake, so most of the cake was left over after that dinner—and it got sent home with me.

I was afraid. I don't keep cake in my house. I couldn't even keep snacks that I slightly liked. If the addiction monster reared up within me, I would consume the entirety of anything within my reach. It never mattered how much was there; I would eat it all in one sitting. When a binge would come on, it felt like an out-of-body experience. I would watch myself make thousands of calories disappear in the matter of minutes in a rush of both panic and euphoria.

But it's what came next that I hated. A tsunami of guilt and shame would sweep in and crush my spirits. Depression and self-hatred would set in as rapidly as the binge itself had begun. I would immediately start mentally planning my workout for the next day, calculating how many extra minutes I would need to be at the gym and how many meals I would need to skip to make up for my sin against my body. This is what I tried to prevent by adhering to strict rules of my making and claiming I didn't even like my favorite foods.

But that day, I found myself with almost an entire cake in my refrigerator.

I didn't know what would happen. Would I be "good" and not eat it? Or would I feel an onset of sadness and then consume it all in one sitting? This dilemma, of course, is not something you can share with *anyone*. The shame of my secret sunk deeply into my identity and darkened every thought I had. With little choice, I acted cool and never even mentioned my fear to my husband. I wanted him to think that I was past all of this.

I put the coconut cake in our downstairs refrigerator, where it wouldn't be something I saw every time, I was in the kitchen. I spent the evening in prayer and the next morning journaling, begging God to show me how to live with cake in my house. Miraculously, I forgot about it.

A few days passed, and I had a craving for something sweet, which made me remember the cake. I cut myself a piece, put the cake back downstairs, and sat down in the kitchen with a plate and a glass of milk. It was everything a piece of cake should be.

Eating it was a piece of cake too. I had one slice and my sweet tooth was satisfied. I wasn't sure what was happening.

I had been praying for freedom from my binge eating for *years*. During this season of my life, the focus of my heart was more on food than it was on God. The more I paid attention to food, the more and more food captured my attention and sucked me into a cycle of constant calculations and contemplations about it. The seemingly unanswered prayers for healing had skewed my faith. I felt like God had been ignoring me. But He hadn't been. He had opened a door, and I was still clutching so tightly to control that I couldn't even see it. Could it be that healing had been available this whole time, and I just hadn't known how to walk in it? Like the Israelites who wandered in the desert for forty years, I had been wandering. Like them, I had been freed and promised a land of milk and honey. But because of my inability to trust and follow God, I was wandering in the desert just outside the Promised Land.

That coconut cake was the start of new beginnings. It was the end of self-flagellation and the pervasive guilt I felt around food. It was the launch of healing, hope, and happiness. With just a small shift of mindset, my world changed. The girl who was afraid of herself around food became the girl who had self-control, freedom, and delight in food.

Food tasted better than ever before. I felt the sweetness

more intensely, and I enjoyed the textures more. I entered a relationship with food that was free from guilt. No longer was I enslaved to the cycle of restriction, binging and shame. Instead, I stepped into a world of tastes, delight, and pleasure I had forgotten even existed. My eyes were opened to an entire world of sweetness and delight God wanted to give me.

Decadent and sweet coconut cake was the tool God used to deliver me from a bondage I feared would hold me down my entire life. His unlikely methods shouldn't surprise me, for when I think about the Promised Land, it is a land of sweetness and creaminess—which is what coconut cake is, after all, isn't it? Finally, I could eat and enjoy dessert. Finally, I could receive and delight in God's love and provision for me.

What is keeping you in the wilderness? What is holding you back from entering the opened gate to the Promised Land that you are circling? Maybe you're like me, and it's a complicated relationship with food, or with drink, or with your body. Or maybe you feel less than because you feel stuck in your career path, your friendships, or your purpose. Whatever is blocking the flow of peace and joy in your life, it's time to stop letting that be the story that comes between you and God's blessings.

I'm encouraged by David's example in the Psalms. He filled his writing with raw emotions, vacillating between delight and absolute joy in the Lord to isolation and being cold, or indifferent. Like me, it seems like he has a hard time *staying* where it's good. Like me, he feels guilty when he's enjoying milk and honey and convinces himself that he is only worthy of broccoli and Brussel sprouts.

At times, I step back into the wilderness. And when I do, it's awful. In the wilderness I am still free, but my spirit isn't prosperous. In the wilderness, I worry about what people think of me. I toss and turn with anxiety at night. I wrestle with a desire for control and a fear of what is coming. I overthink about food and my weight again. In the wilderness, my stress increases and I feel a deep need to prove myself in order to be successful or to have a life of any worth.

To the outsider, my life may look the same in both states. Inside, they are as different of lives as night and day. The difference lies in where I fix my eyes.

In the wilderness, my eyes are on me. God is by my side, but I am leading and forging ahead in my strength. In the Promised Land, God consumes my heart. And though I still struggle with bouts of fear and anxiety, I know I am not alone, and I can feel God lifting the burdens off my heart as they come. I feel light, like a child who is carefree and confidently following the Leader.

The abundant life that God gives us is so good. "The abundant life" doesn't necessarily come with material blessings, financial success, or physical healing but provides strength, peace, and confidence in the Lord's promises and plans for our lives. It is so good that we might even wonder why we ever turn away from it. And yet, we do. I lose my way most often when I'm tired—physically or even more frequently, emotionally. It's hard to live counter-culturally. It's difficult being an optimist in a world of pessimists saturated with negative news. It's difficult to walk away from body bashing, diet talk, and comparison when everyone else does it. It's not cool to pursue a quiet life[53] in a world of internet fame and loud living.

The world tells us to strive and to prove ourselves. God tells otherwise. He sends us out to be light and to be love.[54] He tells us to be in the world, but not of the world.[55] Instead of instructing us to earn good things, He chases us with His goodness and mercy all the days of our lives.[56] He prepared an inheritance for us on this side of Heaven, one in which we would eat and be satisfied.[57]

The world teaches us to wait for the other shoe to drop. It teaches us to sign up for a life of constant competition and comparison. It pressures us to strive and always want more. For many of us, the concept of contentment and satisfaction is foreign. This is exactly why it feels so awkward, so uncertain, and so uncomfortable. But it doesn't have to be, when you know what is promised to you.

So, when your walk in the land of milk and honey feels too good to be true, dig your toes deeper into the sand. No, you don't deserve to be there. Where you sit and what you enjoy is a gift from God—not a reward for what you have done or what you can do, but because you have believed with faith in redemption to the Father's perfect love through the blood of Jesus Christ.

You have found a place of true freedom; since you didn't earn the right to be there, you also can't lose your place there. Once you are free through Christ, you are free indeed.[58]

The blessings and favor of God are too good. That's what delight feels like: too good to be true.

The age-old adage used to ring true to me. I thought you can't have your cake and eat it too. I even used this idea to motivate clients in my personal training business. I would remind them that if they wanted to lose weight, they couldn't also eat cake. The two can't go together: it would be too good to be true.

But you *can* eat cake. You can weather the valleys of life and still live every day with joy. You can walk through financial hardship and still have confidence in knowing God will provide. You can live in a season of hardship and also beauty at the same time. Life *can* be good even when it is bad; and that goodness—or cake—is enjoyed through our perspective of life, not in the circumstance of it.

Cake is good. God is better. And we get to have both in our lives. How lucky are we? The land of milk and honey and coconut cake is available right now to everyone who believes in the promises of God and the hope of Christ. And nothing is sweeter than that.

This land is a lifestyle of inheritance that we have access to today, so straighten your crown, child, and remember that you are royalty in God's kingdom.

CHAPTER 6

Discovering Delight in the Unknown

I stood still, directionless. I didn't know where to go or where to start. It was fifteen years ago, but those few mundane moments at that train station still feel like it was yesterday. It was a summer day in the south of France, and I been traveling for twelve hours. I wasn't in a rush because I had nowhere to go and no one to see. Literally.

I stepped outside of that station in Périgueux with two giant suitcases in hand and paused. I looked left; I looked right. I checked for my passport and verified that the spelling on the train station matched the spelling on the sheet of paper in my hand.

I was in the right place. But I didn't know what to do next.

In a few weeks I would have a job; at least that's what the paper said. In the meantime, I needed a place to sleep and to find a phone to tell my family that I had made it across the ocean safely. This was in the early years of cell phones, when texting didn't really exist, and your phone bill revolved around minutes used. In those dinosaur days of cell phones, international plans weren't a thing and so I had traveled across the world without a plan and without a cell phone.

Money was tight. Taking a job in France was a bit of a financial risk, but it felt right, so I went for it. The promise of adventure was just enough that even though I didn't know how this would play out, I was confident I would stumble upon something wonderful somewhere along the way.

I probably stood frozen outside that train station for twenty minutes. Dozens of travelers and locals swarmed around me, paying me no attention. I needed a plan, and I stood there until I could figure one out. It finally occurred to me to start by finding a place to sleep. Knowing that I couldn't afford a hotel, I started walking in search of a hostel.

I turned in circles and then marched with fake confidence in a direction I hoped would take me toward a hostel. Life is like that sometimes. You know where you are supposed to be, and you have a vague idea of where to go next, but you don't know which direction to take. When that happens, the next right thing to do is simply to do something. Sometimes you just have to start and trust that you can course-correct as you go. For me, that day, that meant just choosing a direction to walk.

And so I walked. With my L.L. Bean duffle bags rolling behind me, my back weighed down with an overstuffed backpack and my hand clutching a little English-French Pocket Dictionary, I ventured onto the narrow streets of the small French town.

I bought a basic cell phone once the cobblestoned streets of *centre ville* led me to stores. The cell phone store was crowded; I had little choice but to leave of my belongings in the street.

Once I had a phone, and I *sort of* understood the contract I had just signed for it, the store employee kindly pointed me and all of my bags toward a place with beds for rent.

The details blend, but within three days of arriving without a plan, I signed a lease for an apartment, confirmed my French cell phone number, found an internet café to email my parents, and walked the streets of my new city. At first, my days were lonely, and my mind stayed exhausted from constant translations. Sooner than expected, though, I found my groove. The once-foreign city became my home. I became a regular at my favorite café, learned where to purchase the best baguette in town, and successfully integrated myself into the community of the small French town.

It all started at that train station and the small step I took into the unknown.

No matter how detailed and airtight our plans may be, we never truly know where our steps will take us. Our human nature wants to have everything figured out, to have a perfect plan. But plans fail, paths get rocky, and the way can be foggy. It can intimidate, but if you are walking with God through conversation, journaling and prayer with Him all that anxiety about the unknown can disappear. This isn't a quick fix, but an invitation into a daily exchange with Him. The Bible tells us to give all our worries to God,[59] for His burden is light[60] and He will sustain us.[61] With Him, everything is *figure-out-able* because He will always teach us the way we should go[62] and provide for all of our needs.[63]

For much of my life, having everything figured out was one of my top priorities. The reality, though, is that life is never like that. Traveling taught me to lean into adventure because when you're in an unfamiliar environment, facing the unknown is really the only choice.

Before my trip to France, I'd always had someone or something to fall back on. But that day was different. I didn't know the language well. I didn't have a phone. I didn't know the town. I didn't have a place to sleep. I didn't know anyone.

Becoming comfortable with not knowing what was ahead, changed me. It forced me to let go of control, to be okay with mistakes and missteps, and to shift my perspective to see life as an adventure, not as a step-by-step roadmap to follow. Spending time far from home taught me to believe in what I could not yet see and to keep walking, sometimes literally, until I got to where I wanted to go. We walk by faith, not by sight, right?[64]

This doesn't come easy to me. I have had to shift my heart intentionally to be thankful for the unfamiliar, the uncertain and the unknown, because y'all, your girl is a control freak. I want to know what comes next, and I want to make sure I'm doing it all right. But I'm a walking contradiction, because I also want to be carefree and like a child. I want to live my days in a way that really shows that I trust the loving eyes and perfect path that God has designed for me.[65]

The year I spent working in France turned out to be one of the best years of my life. It's where I discovered delight or, as the French call it, *joie de vivre* for the first time. I learned that living well is an art form and joy is a choice. I tasted delight through slowing down, eating delicious food, and sharing life with new friends. Everything I experienced was only possible because I took that first step into the unknown when I said "yes" to the job teaching abroad in a small town I couldn't pronounce and to that first step forward at the train station.

Stepping into the unknown doesn't always feel good.

In fact, most of the time it feels like a tornado is sweeping through your mind. It feels overwhelming, like it will knock you over and you won't be able to find your footing. But the only way to find your footing is to take a step forward. It won't feel comfortable, and it won't be easy, but it will deepen your faith and take you where you want to go.

Sometimes this happens in big ways in our lives, and sometimes in unsuspecting ways, like new hobbies. For me, snowboarding has been one of my best teachers.

Shortly after picking up snowboarding as adults, my husband and I were overconfident in our skills. We flew across the country to experience better snow and better slopes. We wanted the real Colorado experience. And we got it, served with a generous side of humility.

We started our trip with friends for a few days at Breckenridge and snowboarding with them boosted our confidence. In those few days, I mastered the basics and gained some speed, so I felt ready for anything. At least I thought I was. I wound up over my head, on a double black diamond at Copper Mountain. To give you an idea of that course's difficulty, Copper is where the U.S. Downhill Ski Team trains.

I'll spare you some details of how I got into this unfortunate position in the first place and skip right to what happened. I was out of my league and stuck on the top of a mountain. The only other people on the mountain that morning were the U.S. Downhill Team members, along with their army of coaches.

I ended up scooting down the entire mountain on my butt—and I cried the whole time. This is awkward to do, and slow, when you have a board attached to both of your feet.

The slope felt so steep and so icy to me that unstrapping my bindings wasn't an option. I was certain that if I did, my board would tumble down the mountain without me and I would roll like an avalanche into a pit of trees off the side of the run.

As I scooted one inch at a time on my butt, internationally ranked skiers clipped past me and around me, yelling things to me about being in their way.

It took me twenty minutes to scoot to the bottom, and by the time I made it to my husband waiting for me at the base, I was a puddle. He hugged me and I slumped in shame. Even though we had just spent a fortune on our full-day lift tickets, I was ready to leave, and we did.

Brandon found the next-closest resort, and we drove there, to Arapahoe Basin. The day turned around for me. Not for Brandon, believe it or not, he actually *broke* his wrist trying to race me down a run. He enjoyed a day of Jack Daniels at the lodge with his arm in a sling and a magnificent view of the Colorado skyline. I enjoyed the powdered hills and redemption from the icy morning.

The day was a bust, expensive and painful in more ways than one, but it's still a day we would never trade, because it was a day of adventure. When I was down, Brandon built me up. And then we flipped the script. We didn't get what we had wanted from the day at all, but we got something better: a good story.

On a day when it seems like everything goes wrong, you can find adventure in looking for what actually went right. Of course, this never feels easy and doesn't come naturally to most of us. That day in the mountains was a botched experience, but the day actually speaks a story of teamwork and exploration. The day speaks of flexibility and openness. The adventure speaks of humility and getting back up once we fall down. It speaks of the view we took in from the top of the mountain basin—where the sky and the peaks extended as far as the eye could see in an embrace of cold pinks, brilliant whites, and subdued blues.

The day wasn't safe, but it was good.

I don't want a life that is safe. Safe doesn't stretch us. Safe doesn't awaken our spirit of adventure. Safe doesn't allow us to step into delight. It doesn't take us to the top of the mountain to beauty so brilliant that it moves our souls. Safe keeps us from needing God in such a way that He can show His love for us through provision and protection when we need it most.

God isn't safe. He is good.[66] He is kind.[67] He is secure.[68] But, safe? No.

Safe implies predictability. God is faithful, but He's not predictable. He doesn't always reveal to us that which we sometimes wished we could know. And He is sovereign. His ways are higher than ours and there will always be things we cannot understand. But when we learn to trust His goodness, we deepen our trust in Him despite all the unknowns. When we trust, we feel safe, even when we don't understand—and that's when we find ourselves ready for adventure.

Even if our discomfort with the unknown is universal, I don't think most of us intentionally remove an adventurous spirit from our lives. As we've discussed, it happens when we value safety and control over God's plan. It also happens as a byproduct of an over-scheduled and distracted culture. And we're the ones missing out. Because, when you remove the spirit of adventure from life, you also reduce your opportunities to the surprise of delight and the connection with God that comes with going on this ride with Him.

An adventurous spirit is fostered little by little, by tasting what life offers. What adventure looks like to you might look different from it looks to me. Adventure isn't limited to just travel, or physical challenges, or a new career. Life is an adventure, and the act of living with your heart open is a super adventure. If your heart is all in, then your feelings will take you on a ride of your life. You'll hear the whispers of what makes your soul sing, and if you're daring enough to go explore that, big things will happen.

For me, writing is an adventure. Writing a book doesn't feel safe. And that's why I like it. It fills me with both joy and terror, which is the perfect recipe for adventure, isn't it?

Second-guessing ourselves, wrestling with doubt, and wondering if we're the only ones who don't really know what we're doing are all signs you're on the path of adventure. Keep going.

The adventure happens in the showing up. Not in the destination of something or the completion of the project. When we embrace the unknown with an openness to adventure, we don't have to get it all right. We can just explore and experiment and rolling with the punches with optimism as we go.

When I write I try on styles, concepts, and chapter structure. I experiment with the thoughts in my heart and exchange them like I'm splattering paint on canvas, trying to achieve the right blend and balance. I taste a word, sometimes a paragraph, and sometimes even a chapter, only to erase it and start over because the taste didn't resonate. And, despite any creative time spent in this process, nothing is ever wasted. The creative process itself is an act of tasting, and no matter the outcome, tasting and seeing is achievement.

Sometimes, our adventures are experiences that open us up to feeling and being led by the Spirit. Learning to listen to God's guidance, and then step into it, is a lifelong adventure. What delights my heart is knowing that where I go, the Spirit goes with me. And, since where the Spirit of the Lord is, there also is freedom,[69] then I know that wherever I go, I will be good. I know whatever will happen, I will have access to peace.

And what a promise we have in that. To know that the Lord will never leave me, and that He will lead me gives me an unshakeable[70] peace. With God, the unknown is always safe.

When we avoid adventure and the unknown, we fool ourselves out of the life we are meant to live. We settle for a semi-version of life, copying what everyone else is doing, instead of going all in on the unknown that would make our heart sing. Many of us settle for just getting by because we think it's what we've been assigned. The thing is, we will never know what is really available to us until we step outside of what feels safe. If you've ever felt an ache for something more, for a life that feels more meaningful, then you already know God is calling you to step into the unknown. The question is, will you do it?

The ache can feel confusing sometimes. I know, because I feel it too. I feel it when I have a strong sense of purpose, but the actualization of that dream feels confusing and vague. I feel it when the straight line I was walking turns curvy and I can't see if the path ahead ends with a fall over the edge of a cliff or a glorious mountaintop view. I feel it when I'm conflicted in my faith—wavering between unshakeable hope in God's promises and despair that I am going to trip up over my own feet as I walk in the dark of the unknown.

And then I remember the adventure of it all. If I knew

every step ahead of me, I would get lost in the future and miss out on the present. I would miss out on the character development, the beauty, and the confidence that comes when I trust the Director of my adventure. I wish that my heart didn't ache with fear and uncertainty in those moments, but I'm glad that it does. The ache is a gift.

That conflict I feel reminds me of my need. It brings me to my knees. It humbles my heart—the controlling, self-sufficient part of it—into a place of surrender. I remember that I'll never know exactly what is ahead of me, but I have to seek someone beyond myself to guide me. The ache leads me back to Him. It brings me confidence and blessing,[71] and therefore I don't need to know what is ahead, for I already know that I will have all that I need.

The ache aligns our heart with the God of the universe. It reminds us we have big choices to make each day. We can choose to live in the truth of God's refuge and allow Him to guide us along the path He's laid for us. Or we can keep walking along in our own strength, hoping that our feet will be secure where we step. The choice is ours, and both options are risky. If we're going to have to bet on someone, and we can't avoid the unknown, we are better off to bet on God than on ourselves.

It is in the unknowns of our lives that God does His greatest work in us. In those areas He stretches us, He develops us, and He teaches us to trust in Him. It is also in those places He uses us to be light to others who are in the dark with us. We need the unknown, and those in the unknown need us to be there, alongside them, too.

It's time to get off the sidelines of life and dare to delight in the life God has given you—even when you can't yet see the full picture or have all the answers. Yes, it will feel risky, but you're needed in the game.

Let's leave the familiar and let our faith guide our steps. We don't know what is ahead, but we know who is. He is good, His plans for us are good, and the work He is doing in our hearts as we learn to believe just how much He loves us is good. We have nothing to fear—He will make our path straight[72] and our steps secure[73]—so let's chase adventure and show the world just how alive we are because of our God's love.

CHAPTER 7

Discovering Delight Through Doing Less

’ve got a stubborn streak in me—something I never realized until I became the owner of the world's most stubborn dog. Finnegan is an Irish Terrier, a breed known for being bull-headed. They warned us about his tenacity, but we thought it would be endearing.

When Finn was a puppy, he wanted to be boss. I enrolled him in puppy school, where I was coached on how to stand firm and make sure he knew I was his pack leader. Even so, I would take him for walks and, midway down a trail, he would sit down and decide the walk was done. Or that we were going the wrong direction. He became immovable, like a little doggie statue. Sure, I could move him, but to do it, I had to drag him, or just pick him up and carry him. Either way, I looked like a fool and he was still winning.

This obstinate dog became a mirror of my own stubborn nature. He thinks he knows best. He gets ideas about the direction he wants to take, and he won't let them go. He is narrow-focused and hard to convince otherwise. He has strong preferences. I am not very different.

I spent most of my life telling God what my plans were. I had specific directions I wanted to take and assumed that God would follow my lead. And the entire time, I had no idea how stubborn and small-minded I was being.

My stubbornness doesn't just stop there. I was born with a drive to push myself. It didn't come from my parents or anyone else; it was just a part of me. Wired to be a workaholic and over-achiever, I stubbornly committed to doing more than was needed in an effort to prove myself and make my own way.

When I was ten, I pushed myself so hard in swim practices I ended up at the cardiologist for extensive testing for heart acceleration and palpitations. The results came back inconclusive, but the doctors told my coaches I needed to slow down.

Try to stop trying, they told me, which was an upside-down concept that I simply couldn't wrap my head around. My coaches made me sit out of some workout sets and tried to teach me about the value of varied speeds, varied effort, rest, and recovery, but I was having none of it. I wanted to go all out all the time. It was the only way I thought I would ever stand out from the crowd. And I needed to stand out.

I am a worker. I thrive on trying. I take pride in knowing that I am willing to out-train anyone. If I needed to work on a technique to improve my speed, I'd get to the pool an hour before practice to do a thousand repetitions of that one thing. If I needed more endurance, I would trade sleep for time on the treadmill and run until I couldn't any longer. If I needed to have a mental edge on my competitors, I would train when I was sick, even if that meant throwing up on the pool deck.

I didn't believe in rest.

Rest was for wimps, and the light-hearted. I was neither. I leaned into determination with fear that without it, I would be a failure, and unlovable. This drove me to keep up a relentless pace to prove myself in the world.

Unsurprisingly, my pride caused my fall. My inability to chill out and trust my training stunted my potential. I spun my wheels and stayed stagnant. The only thing my obsession with hard work got me was exhaustion, frustration, and disappointment. The harder I tried, and the more I did, the worse I got at everything I did and the louder the critical voice in my mind became.

The anxiety I experienced was familiar, and so I stayed comfortable there in my discomfort. I made things so hard for myself that I actually feared what might happen if they became easy. Letting life be easier felt, well, hard. It meant I would have to let go of my feigned sense of control and allow anything to happen. That scared me to my core.

In order to stop trying so hard, to find peace with doing less, I had to go back to the very basics of my beliefs. I had to look at what had God said about me. I relearned that He said I lacked nothing,[74] and that I was a masterpiece.[75] I saw He said rest was not only good, but commanded. It opened my eyes to a God who invites me into abundance, peace, and glory. It awakened my soul—and honestly, surprised me—to remember that He doesn't just love me, but He also sings over me and delights in the details of my day.[76] And to top it all off, I realized that this entire process is not about perfection, but progression. God is still doing a work in me[77]—so I can be confident in where I am today, even if it's not yet where I want to be, for He is still transforming me, taking me where

I need to go.

Thankfully, God sees through our stubbornness and meets us in fresh, personal ways. For me, He used my love of travel to move and change my heart. I had been praying for God to do a new thing in my heart. I was restless in my habits and exhausted from the constant hustle of an over-committed life. And then He plopped me right in the middle of a pastoral paradise.

International travel with young children is a challenge, but because Brandon and I value travel so much, we made it happen. Driving to our Scotland rental home in Blaich Highlands felt like we were driving through a postcard itself. The single-track road led our rental car five miles down its remote and narrow path. The road danced dangerously close to the edge of the lapping loch on the left and the edge of the mountain slope on the right. Pockets of bright green pasture interspersed themselves, freckled with flocks of sheep. Our mountain cottage was worth the perilous journey. With a wraparound porch, freely roaming sheep, and majestic views of the loch with Munro peaks boasting behind it, it was quintessentially Scottish.

The first morning I went out for my run and encountered a traffic jam of sheep in the middle of the road. They didn't move and didn't show any interest in moving. I slowed to a walk along the foggy shoreline and found myself within a fingertip's reach of their wool. Eventually they looked bothered, and then, in a rather unexpected move, they *ran* along the street *with* me. Some veered into the grass to continue their breakfast, but a few carried on in front of me—at an astonishing clip—for a few hundred yards. I continued running, passing several other flocks with each mile, each flock interacting with me in their own unique way. When I circled back past the original flock as I finished my run, their eyes lit up in recognition, and they didn't even move. I interpreted it as a friendly nod from the neighborhood that I was welcome.

The sheep were not who I thought they were. These guys weren't stupid or slow. They ran upwards of a six-minute mile as they scooted in front of me, and they moved as a pack, clearly favoring the value of community and connection. A little internet research taught me that sheep have an almost 360-degree vision and incredible facial recognition and memory of sheep and humans alike.

Over the following days my runs were similar, each one earning me more favor with the flocks. And as I ran, the water of the loch lapping upon the shore and the curves of the single-track lane opening up to still subsidiaries circled by brilliantly green grass, my spirit stirred. I was almost literally running through the manifestation of the twenty-third Psalm.[78]

It was hard to not stop running and just do what my soul was craving: to lie down beside still waters. As I ran, soaking in this pocket of peace tucked away from the world, I decided that those sheep had it made. I simply couldn't imagine a more pristinely beautiful place in the world to be a sheep. Those sheep lacked nothing. As soon as I thought that I felt the same. I felt peace come upon my heart and I felt at home, right there along with those sheep. It was the first time that I felt honest in saying, "The Lord is my shepherd, I lack nothing."

As I considered those sheep, I hungered for peace in a way I had never before. God really was making me lie down in green pastures. I didn't think I wanted the green pastures; I was too busy trying to be successful and seen. I went to Scotland to write and be productive. God took me to Scotland to remove me from my world and show me that His plan was better than mine.

The entire week was a gentle sabbatical from our normal, modern life. I woke to coffee on the cabin porch and roosters calling. We took family walks in our Wellington boots, the children running ahead in fields of flowers. We poured wine at night and played music as we let our children stay up hours past their bedtimes merely because they were giggling with delight in their little world of made-up games. It was simple, and profound, and soul changing. I was still working in the margins—fixing website crashes on my site, responding to customer service complaints in my inbox, and keeping up with a few clients—but that stress barely registered as white noise in the atmosphere of peace that surrounded me.

While I was in the Highlands, I felt a nudge from God. This wasn't just a little vacation. What I was feeling wasn't meant to be a quaint little experience. Instead, my heart knew that what I was craving wasn't a mere fantasy, but actually an invitation. Rest, after all, isn't a suggestion; it's a command from the One who made us. I'm good at following instructions and am disciplined at whatever I put my mind to, so I like to think of myself as an obedient person. But when I got honest about my obedience about rest, I couldn't deny I'd been deliberately turning away from God's call to balance and sabbath.

Even after this incredible, eye-opening experience, I still fight the idea of slowing down. I fight it hard—hard enough that in order to move forward in obedience, I need an accountability system to force myself to rest. I hire coaches, I work with therapists, and I confide in my friends to keep me straight. The temptation to open my email throughout the day literally calls out to me like a siren. My running shoes look lonely when I'm taking a day of physical rest, and I have the tendency to rate the quality of my day based on the amount of money I made, the quantity of steps I have taken, or the number of items ticked off on my to-do list.

Once I finally had the courage to rest, I loved it—and I wanted more of it. In fact, I felt God nudging me to do even less, but I resisted. I was afraid of letting go and truly living a slower life. It would be opposite of anything I had ever previously known. Still, I knew I needed to downshift *everything*. And despite my childish resistance, I felt God's patience with me as I tiptoed my way toward change. I understood He was prompting me in particular about two areas of my life: my exercise and my work. Both held my heart's affection, and both needed my surrender. I didn't want to do it.

My normal ninety-minute workouts needed to become seventy-five minutes long instead, and my sixty-minute workouts needed to be shortened to forty-five minutes. Thoughts of fear raced through my head. *What if I didn't work out enough? Would I gain weight? Would that fifteen minutes really make a difference? This is stupid. I'll just stick to what I'm doing—or should I?*

God wasn't after my time, or even my fitness level. He was after my heart. I was addicted to the structure and control I got from my workout routine. It kept me safe. It protected my anxieties and fears from revving up and it was where I cast all my cares. And it worked, for short bursts of time at least. I would feel better, but then the anxiety would bubble back up and back to the altar of the treadmill I would go to surrender my worries.

I knew God had a better way for me. In fact, one of the first Bible verses I had memorized as a kid in Sunday School was about casting my cares on the Lord.[79] I knew what I was supposed to do; I just did not know how to do it. I found myself stuck between knowing something is available and actually knowing how to access it. And since I didn't know who to talk to about it, or even how to put it into words, I buried it in my mind under the label of not being spiritual enough.

Sometimes, though, the problem isn't that we're not spiritual enough, smart enough, capable, or chosen—it's that we need a little help truly understanding and accepting that which we have been promised. I realized that I didn't actually want to give my cares to God—not because I didn't think He would take them, but because I didn't think He actually cared about me. Though I believed in God's power and salvation through His Son, I still thought God was too big and busy for me and my small problems. So instead of handing them over to a distant God, I put a band-aid on my anxieties through productivity, exercise, and staying busy. I thought it was the only way I could live.

Though I'd heard differently that God cares about each of us, I didn't know how to access that truth for my own life. But that's the thing about God's love: He has given everything—even His own son—to make sure every one of us can reach it. Sometimes, like my young son trying to reach candy on a tall shelf, we just need to find a stepping stool.

A stool gives us a boost. It shortens the distance between what we want and where we are. And, contrary to my original belief, the "stool" to access the grace of God isn't a big step. Convinced I needed to work harder, I thought the stool was a jump. I tried to make myself bigger, tougher, more self-disciplined, more resilient—whatever "more" would be to help me "be better." The stepping stool to grace is not in doing more, though; it's found in doing less. In slowing down to savor life and grace. It's found not in stressing and struggling to do more, but in slowing down and surrendering. I found the stepping stool to grace lying in green pastures. In taking naps. In trusting the Shepherd.

Surrender is the step that renders all things accessible. And God will keep us in a holding pattern of exhaustion, frustration, and disappointment until we change our strategy and understand that God is not after our performance; He is after our hearts.

He was after my faith.

He was after my will.

He was after my surrender.

When I finally released the things I'd been holding onto—security found in success, control through achievement, belief that I had to earn God's attention and favor—I discovered peace I can only remember feeling as a young, carefree girl. It's the peace that I breathed in deeply in the Highlands, surrounded by sheep and casually drinking coffee on a hillside covered in wildflowers.

What I've learned is that when I do less, God does more. That doesn't mean that I don't do what I am supposed to do. It just means that I'm learning to stop and trust God when it's time to rest.

It is scary, but the less I try to force my success, the more doors God opens for me. The less I stress about what I look like, the more beautiful I actually feel. The less I worry about what people think, the more radiantly alive I ultimately feel. It's true, what they say, less is really more.

Doing less may feel ridiculously uncomfortable. This is not just one day of rest, or a day binge watching Netflix on the couch when you're sick. This is a lifestyle shift, and one that is countercultural to the world. Eventually, as you accept the gift of peace that God has extended, though, you'll settle into this space with the joy that God created us for. It's Heaven that has come to Earth. It's the taste of what we were created for—where we were originally put—in the garden. Our hearts are wired for this place, this beauty, and this piece of paradise.

I pushed back on God's promptings for less in my life. Sometimes it was because I was addicted to the business and rush of life. Other times because I feared what slowing down might actually look like or make me miss. Ultimately, I didn't trust God to be good.

In fact, I pushed back on God's love for most of my life because it seemed too good to be true. In a world of conditional love and broken relationships, I harbored deep cynicism. I had put God in a box, imagining Him to be small and distant. I had convinced myself that He was disappointed in me as much as I was disappointed in myself.

As the theologian A. W. Tozer once said, "What comes into our minds when we think about God is the most important thing about us…"[80] I had spent most of my time thinking about myself, not about God, so of course my view of Him was distorted.

Scotland changed things for me. The week I spent at that cabin in the Highlands with my family, running the foggy mornings alongside the flocks and listening to the crickets' chirp in the loch's brush at the fall of night, my soul turned inside out. I knew God was doing a deep thing in me, but every night when I sat down to write after the children went to bed, my mind was blank. All day long my body had pulsed with inspiration and big ideas, but at night, my thoughts were blank.

I closed my laptop every night, barely a word written, which doesn't speak well for a writing retreat, and I read and reread Psalm 23. He *makes* me lie down in green pastures.

Finally, I got it. God wasn't just pointing me to some of David's most famous words; He was making me live them out. I wasn't productive there. I was present. I wasn't rushed. I roamed the green fields, cup of coffee in hand. I wasn't distracted with comparison, overwhelm, or performance. I had all that I needed and more beauty and peace than I ever knew possible.

The taste of green pastures made my soul hunger for more. I think I hear your soul grumbling with hunger too. You may not need to travel across an ocean to find your green pastures. God is inviting you to rest right now. Your rest might not look like shorter workouts or a week in the mountains for you. Perhaps it looks like putting boundaries on your email, saying "no" to too many commitments, or taking more leisurely walks outside with your family.

Whatever it looks like, when you see it, slow down for it. It's time to rest and taste the goodness that God has prepared for you. You're a daughter of the King, you have the time to rest and the access to the green pastures, so settle in and give it a try.

CHAPTER 8

Discovering Delight in Dead Ends

D ead ends give me mixed emotions. If I'm out for a run, they make for a nice turnaround spot for my route. If I'm with my kids on bikes, we spend an extra ten minutes playing at the end of the street—free from the worry of cars. But if I'm in a car myself, lost somewhere new, and the road just dead ends? Well, that's when my feelings change. It feels too much like the times in life when I think my life is going one way, only to find that the path I'm following abruptly ends and leaves me feeling unhinged.

To be honest, most of my life has felt like that last scenario. It's like the time Brandon crashed his Jeep into an unexpected dead-end as he drove south to the beach late at night. He was driving on a highway—no other cars around, as everyone else had exited for another route.

There were probably some road construction signs that he missed. After all, he'd had a long day, starting at 4:30 a.m. for a full day of work, then a drive home that put him on the road to South Carolina at 11 p.m. As he describes it, the road just stopped. Yes, the entire highway. His Jeep smashed into the construction barricades that formed a fence across both lanes, causing severe damage.

But it wasn't as bad as it could have been. We still don't know how he missed the exit ramps and rerouting detour, but those concrete barricades saved Brandon's life. The highway's temporary dead end was right at the start of a bridge that was under construction. Without those barricades, Brandon would have driven unsuspectingly into the water at 70 miles per hour. The dead end saved his life.

We might not like dead ends, but if looked at through the right lens, we might find that they are gifts from a good Father who wants to protect us with turnaround points of grace and salvation.

Dead ends can be places of praise. They don't always feel this way to start, but without fail, He covered my dead ends in protection and love. Underneath the pain, the frustration, and the overwhelm that comes in a dead end, we can find goodness.

You might not call the dead ends of your life dead ends. You might just describe it as feeling stuck or as just struggling. Whether you call it a dead end or call it stuck, we have all been there. Sometimes we are lost, and we know it, but other times we don't even realize we've lost our way until it feels too late, like Brandon in his Jeep.

The dead ends in life can be defining moments. How we got there isn't as important as what we will do to move on and move forward. The problem is that when stuck, it's human nature to obsess over how it happened. We look for people to blame. We deep dive into the circumstantial evidence. We try to analyze the decisions we made that got us there.

When Brandon called that night and told me of the accident, I was frantic, trying to understand how he missed all the signage and how fast he was going. I had questions that couldn't be answered—and, ultimately, those questions didn't matter. What mattered was that he was stuck in the middle of nowhere, in the middle of the night and with little sleep. He needed help, and he needed rest.

The same goes for us.

When we find ourselves stuck—or someone we love finds themselves stuck—there's no need to over-analyze what got us there. We're there, and that's that. What matters is that we ask ourselves how to stop moving in circles and instead move forward in a better direction.

Sometimes, though, people just stay put. The over-analysis of how they got there, and the intimidation of how they will get out of there, is paralyzing. It doesn't need to be.

God has filled the Bible with story after story of redeemed dead ends. Those dead ends—from Joseph being sold into slavery by his brothers,[81] to Daniel being thrown in a den with hungry lions,[82] to David killing Uriah to cover up adultery,[83] to the outcast woman at the well at midday in the desert sun,[84] to the woman with a bleeding problem who was unclean and unwanted[85]—all seem hopeless and messy. But as you read, the impossible in their stories becomes possible when God takes over. He is the God of the turnaround. He is the God who makes smooth a rocky path. He is the God who secures our footing on the side of a cliff. He is the God who specializes in taking insurmountable circumstances and turning them into a miraculous turning point of healing, transformation, and victory.

I want that kind of story in my life too.

I have had my fair share of dead ends—from the ones that seem impossible to avoid to the ones I could have surely made better decisions to avoid—but when I started inviting God into them, rather than feeling stuck like a victim in them, things changed. When we invite God into our dead ends, those dead ends turn into places of delight and deliverance.

At first, I didn't believe this to be entirely true. Some dead ends feel, well, too dead. It's easy to read the stories of the Bible and believe that God comes through for those heroes. As I investigated my dead ends, it occurred to me I believed in two gods. I believed in the God of the Bible, and I celebrated how He showed up for those people. But, in my own life, I believed in a watered-down, disinterested, and distant God— like a knock-off version of the biblical God I so deeply loved. I was perpetuating some of what was keeping me stuck, and so I couldn't imagine that God would still want to help free me.

The thing is, God is immutable, which means unchangeable. How He was then is how He is now. It is literally His nature. So, when we read the Bible and see His faithfulness, His trustworthiness, His power, and His personalized love for His people, we can read that and know that He has not changed.

He sees our dead ends and He can turn them around. But we have to invite Him into them, which means we have to stop holding onto our guilt and shame and trying to fix ourselves. He meets us in those places, does miraculous things, and shows off His power and might.

I'm going to go as far as saying that when we invite God in, our dead ends fill with delight. God doesn't just rescue us; He revives and revitalizes us. And how beautiful is that? That the Creator of all things would slow down to find us, be with us, and rescue us is an intimate expression of great delight.

The dead ends of life are the life-changing parts of our story. Sometimes we are so caught up in them we miss out on how God is circling around us, waiting for an invitation in. I didn't invite God into my dead ends until I became desperate for his help.

God doesn't simply show up in our dead ends, He meets us there with excessive kindness. I didn't always see it this way. Actually, when I felt stuck, I felt like He had turned His back on me. I thought I had been abandoned.

But He hadn't turned away. In fact, He never left my side. I just didn't see Him because I was looking in all the wrong places. Dead ends are like that. They steal our attention and make us feel like we're the only ones struggling and stuck with no proper way out.

I'm not sure what your dead ends look like, but my guess is that in me sharing mine, we will have some overlapping experiences. I hope you see that a dead end is nothing more than an invitation to a better path and a place where God's greatest miracles take place.

When I was in my twenties, I followed a man instead of following Jesus. He told me he loved me; he told me I was chosen. Desperate for validation, I did what he asked. I sold everything I owned, from my furniture to my car. He convinced me I wouldn't need anything that he and I couldn't build in life together. It would be us against the world.

I gave him my purity, and he took over control of me. He made an empty promise, and I believed it even after he broke it repeatedly. He promised me love, so when that love looked like abuse, I didn't question it. He knew better than me, so I must have deserved it. He moved me away from my family and picked my friends for me. He laughed at my ideas and dreams and told me that every woman wanted to be me—not because of anything to do with *me,* but because every woman wanted to be with *him.* Together we built a life of lies, ones that I believed myself in my life of isolation.

I gave up on my persistent pursuit of Jesus. Instead, I felt temporarily fulfilled in the praise this man and I received from the world. People called us *the "it couple."* Together we looked like Ken and Barbie. We threw parties for ourselves, paid massive bar tabs to be ostentatious, drove a car we couldn't afford, tanned and exercised obsessively, and lived together with a goal to make other people jealous. We thought we were happy, that this was the good life.

Behind closed doors, things looked different. Had anyone seen what was really happening behind the facade of perfection, they would have seen something different. There were household items thrown in anger, drunken threats shouted, police incidents of domestic violence, drugs flushed down toilets, and tears—lots and lots of tears.

I had put my faith in a man instead of in God.

It didn't seem as clear cut as that when it happened. Before I ever met this man, I had harbored unbelief. The weight of unanswered prayers had weakened my faith. I had been faithful to God my entire life, but it didn't seem to matter. I felt like God didn't hear me. I thought everyone else had life figured out, everyone *but* me. It seemed that *other* people were achieving the things I dreamed of and the ones I still prayed for. And furthermore, my Christian friends who had saved themselves for marriage met godly husbands in college and started their dream lives together at 22. I felt forgotten, and as the months and years passed, I felt more and more overlooked. The more I felt forgotten, the more resentment I felt for the decisions I had made to put my faith first.

God had overlooked me; I was certain He had turned a blind eye to the cries of my heart. I didn't think He would come through for me, so I made my own way. I met my ex-fiancé and followed him with faith. I was going to answer my own prayers and create a new timeline, because waiting on God wasn't working for me anymore.

A few years passed, and life was bad. Like many suffering domestic abuse, I didn't want to leave. He didn't mean to hurt me, I believed. He promised he would start getting help, going to meetings, and he even threw around the idea that maybe we could find a church to go to together. The promise was just enough to keep me hooked. After all, he was simply recovering from the abuse he experienced as a child. He didn't mean to be so mean.

I didn't even realize that I was living a dead end. I painted a picture of a happy, luxurious life in the big city. I made sure my old friends saw the pictures and parties. I lied to my family.

Eventually, though, his lies compounded, and the drugs didn't disappear. Alcohol fueled chaos in our lives, and I spent most of my nights alone, wondering where my fiancé was and why he didn't come home at night. I threw pillows against walls and cried myself to sleep. I hid in this world for months until eventually I couldn't hide anymore. My brother and his wife visited for New Year's Eve in Chicago, and it was disastrous. It's hard to keep the story alive when the lies are so clear; so, I broke off the engagement.

I spent days crying. I wept on the plane ride home and continued to cry myself into depression as I moved back into my parents' house. It was bleak. I was broke, blurry-eyed, and bent up over the ghost of the promised life I thought I was going to live. I didn't know who I was anymore. I just knew that I was stuck, and my prospects didn't look hopeful.

God saw something different in the dead end.

He saw a place for healing and rebuilding. An opportunity to upend the lies I had told and begin rebuilding my relationship with my family. He saw the godly, encouraging friends and mentors that He would bring into my life as co-workers. These are the people who would invite me back to church, back into the Word, and back to seeing God as someone for me, not against me. In the last place I wanted to be on Earth—the dead end of my hometown—God made a place of rebirth.

He rescued me from the path I had chosen, and used Fredericksburg, Virginia, as a place to reset me. In that place He gave fresh breath to my confidence, my community, and my calling. And, against all odds, it was also where He positioned me to go on a blind date with the man who would become my husband.

God uses our dead ends as turnarounds. He is the God who brings dead things alive.

Another dead end felt more like a sinkhole I'd never escape. I had never known anyone who got out of this particular dead end, the one that pulled me in, held me down, and tried to swallow me up.

The doubly frustrating thing about being a Christian with an eating disorder is that you know that what is consuming you is of no eternal value. The very struggle itself turns you into a hypocrite of the soul, and that conviction crumbles the confidence that was already wavering in your heart.

I *knew better* than to worry about my body. I also knew better than to abuse it as I did, for how we treat our bodies is how we treat the temple of the holy spirit of God. The more I fought to fix myself—to stop wanting to use food to numb myself and to stop relying on workouts to manage my anxiety—the worse my addiction became. The sink hole got stickier. The more I thought about food, the more it controlled me. I circled around the same five pounds, gaining and losing it, with my identify, worth and beauty riding on it, for years on end. Whether your struggle is with a few pounds or many, your too-long limbs or short stature, the color of your hair or the way your nose looks, the inability to see ourselves as beautiful as we are is one of the enemy's most effective tactics to fill us with unworthiness.

It was like a riding a bike vigorously around in circles in a cul-de-sac and wondering why you aren't actually getting any further down the street. I couldn't break the cycle because, unlike drugs or alcohol, you can't just quit food, and I didn't know how else to think about it.

Feeling stuck can make you desperate. I used to fantasize about being deathly sick—only temporarily, long enough to break my habits but not long enough to hurt me. I wanted to get my nutrition through tubes and to rest my body in a hospital bed. I didn't want to think about food anymore. The pace I kept and compulsive exercise I engaged in were killing me. I felt hopeless, and I stayed there, downcast in the dead end of my disorder for more than a decade.

I measured my value and my worthiness daily in the mirror. My stomach was the governing deity, and it ruled with a fickle fist.

It was a dead end of vanity, pride, and a misunderstanding of beauty. I felt unremarkable, unnoticeable, unmemorable. Previously I was known for what I did—for what I accomplished in the pool and in school. My discipline needed to be above reproach—fiercer and more committed than anyone else I knew, for that would make me better than them, and I needed to be the best.

In that sinkhole my desire to be the best and to stand out from others destroyed me. I traded in my confidence in how God created me in exchange for a belief that I was broken, less than, and a mistake. The weight of feeling unremarkable deepened the distance I felt between myself and God, largely because I was angry about how He created me.

I spent my days envious of other body types, convinced they were more beautiful—and therefore more loveable—than me. I was incredibly jealous of people who walked on the beach with confidence as I had to force myself into wearing bathing suits in public—and still faced a nonstop chorus of self-critical thoughts when I did. I wanted less muscle, longer legs, a flatter chest, a higher metabolism, and thinner hair. I wanted to be anyone other than myself in my body. I disliked my body so intensely that I strategically avoided mirrors, even ones I had to stand in front of to wash my hands.

Of course, the intensity of my struggle matched the intensity of the secrecy I kept about my struggle. I stuffed these anxieties deep down and used them as fuel to drive the fire of striving, self-improvement, and weight loss that consumed my attention. I spent any spare emotional energy pretending that I was happy, carefree, and confident. The entire thing was dreadfully lonely, and I never imagined that anyone—especially not God—would understand or have compassion on the crazy cycle where I found myself stuck.

I was dead inside, and my body was the problem. I couldn't run away from it, because where I went, there I was. I was a walking pile of dry bones.

I didn't know it then, but God specializes in bringing dry bones to life. He puts breath into what has no breath, and life and vibrancy into what someone has ripped apart, ravished, and rotted.[86]

For ten years I prayed for healing from my eating disorder. And for ten years God said, "not yet"—or at least *I thought* He had. Again, I felt angry and overlooked, finding myself living in the dead ends of life. The thing is, God *had* granted me healing but because it didn't look the way I expected, I missed it.

I had expected God would erase my desire to comfort myself with food. Or perhaps heal me with an inexplicable, miraculous metabolism shift that finally gave me the body I wanted. I was waiting for a mind free from ever having to think about food again—but that didn't happen. I chalked it up as unanswered prayer and accepted that I would always struggle with food and with my body. I embraced my addictions and disorders as part of life, and just how it was going to be.

Food was the friend I needed when no one else seemed safe and my drug of choice when I wanted an escape. It was how I played god in my world, feigning a sense of control over my universe by manipulating calories and macronutrients. A toxic and flawed system, it swallowed me up into its cycle of restriction, overdose, wash and repeat repeatedly. For years I admonished myself for my lack of willpower or discipline to break my patterns. I punished myself for not being able to snap out of it and to "just be good."

I wanted out of the hell I was in, but I didn't believe I could get out. And on my own, I couldn't.

I had a misplaced faith. It wasn't faith in God, but faith in myself. I was convinced that if I could fix myself, then I would be happy. If I could make my body perfect, then I would be beautiful. If I could achieve more things, then I would be important. I worked my faith out in proving myself, competing, and self-improvement—an unquenchable cycle that always left me thirsting for more.

And yet, even though I circled that same dead end for years, God was still at work. Over time God introduced people, mentors, and programs into my life that gave me confidence I never had. As the seeds of confidence were watered, they grew and grew, and what started as slight shifts of thinking became bondage-breaking behavior change. The differences were slight, though, so I initially missed them as the answer to prayer that they were.

Then, one day I woke up, looked in the mirror and felt beautiful. The compliments my husband gave me felt real, and I believed them. What was once dead in me felt alive; my dry bones had breath and life again. A decade of tiny miracles pieced themselves together in that lightbulb moment when I finally felt my thinking click and change.

Finally, I could see that no amount of weight loss or make-up or eyelash extensions will make me feel beautiful enough. I had starved, abused, and exercised myself to exhaustion for years and no matter what, I always wanted more. The finish line of physical perfection kept moving. It always does. God pulled me out of that dead end, though, pointing me back to the truth that I am wonderfully made, created by Him for good works and beloved no matter what the mirror ever tells me. After years of keeping myself trapped in that dead end, God had reached in and rescued me—not in the way I expected, but in a way that healed and delighted me.

We are told that God's goodness runs after us, which feels foreign when the darkness of a dead end is all you can see. The way out starts by looking for any light that you can find. You will find it in God's Word, in the embrace of a friend, and in any place where we reach out for help and connection. The isolation of a dead end creates deep disconnection within us, making the darkness feel heavier than it actually is.

But when we step out of that isolated narrative, and connect with others to help pull us out, we see that we are not alone at all. We will see that His goodness and mercy follow us all the days of our life[87] and His presence goes before and behind us wherever we go,[88] then the shadows are simply evidence of God's light shining through the surrounding darkness.

Your shadows and your setbacks might not be as dark of places as they seem to be. If you look, you might just find that God is waiting for you in them, ready to show up and show off as He takes what feels impossible and does it for you. And yes, He will do it, because He doesn't just merely love you, He delights in you, His child and His masterpiece.[89]

CHAPTER 9

Discovering Delight in Emotions

I have always been the "emotional" one in my family. I hated it. My emotions were all over the place and I felt like a black sheep. Everyone else seemed able to stay cool as cucumbers and I would cry at the drop of a dime. I felt all things—good and bad—deeply. I felt branded by my sensitivity and worked hard to pretend it didn't bother me.

Someone close to me once called me "crazy" for being too emotional. They said it nonchalantly, but it caused my imagination to spiral. I convinced myself that I would spend my life alone, unfit for society. I simply was too much of a crybaby to be functioning in this world. I was an over-the-top emotional kid, in a very pragmatic family. I didn't fit.

Around the age of eight, when my athletic talent became apparent, I leaned in hard to being an athlete. It made me feel like less of a black sheep. I learned that if I used all my emotional energy toward training and competition that I would be too tired to be "too emotional" in other areas of my life. It worked, mostly.

I ended up teaching myself to be busy *all the time*. If I was busy, then I could keep my emotions at bay. As a result, I created a life for myself in which I'm not very good at sitting still. Then, God matched me with a husband who is opposite to me in all the right ways. When we first met, I didn't think the relationship could work. Brandon goes through life at a leisurely pace. He is present and unrushed. A total type B, he is never trying to prove himself or make a scene to stand out. It was a miracle he had the patience to pursue someone with a frazzled energy and distracted focus as me, but he stuck with me.

Largely thanks to Brandon, I have gotten better at slowing down. Not a lot better, but a little better; I'm going for progression, friends, not perfection. My breakthrough came as a byproduct of the marital tension we had in our first few years of marriage. The only fights we had been about how to use our time. I wanted us to do more and more, and he wanted us to do less and less. I thought staying busy and filling up every hour of our weekends with activity would make us happy. He believed that prioritizing rest, living intentionally, and having free time to use for creativity was what we needed.

Brandon stayed firm, and after five years of resisting his way of doing things, his influence wore off on me in a positive way. I over-schedule less and force myself to stop and smell the roses—or more accurately, to be patient as my kids stop and make wishes on white dandelions.

That said, my relaxed pace is still what some people consider speed walking, I get bored taking baths. I am a multi-screen multi-tasker when we are watching TV. I run a business from home while doing life with toddlers and am typically always training for a marathon or endurance event to fill up my free time. I am attracted to doing too much and to doing it quickly. One thing, however, has always gotten me to stop and slow down with my full attention: movies.

Movies make me stop. They pull me in, and I sit on the couch, allowing myself to rest and get fully engaged in the story. Ever since my daughter was two years old, we've made pizza movie nights a family tradition. Friday nights are the one evening we all know what to expect. Cheese pizza, a movie on Netflix, family time in pajamas, and all four of us wedged in together on the couch.

One recent Friday, we watched *Ugly Dolls,* an animated movie about overcoming perfectionism, the pressures of society, weirdness and the deep desire to belong. In the movie, the dolls realize they don't have to be perfect in order to be loved by children. A sucker for animation with an emphasis on life lessons—especially the lesson that we're all beautiful on the inside, I had been excited to show this movie to my daughter since it was first released.

Toward the end of the movie, the main character acts in love, selflessly comforting another instead of attempting to win a competition. As we watched, snuggled up on the couch, my daughter climbed off my lap and sat upright. In a somewhat startled voice, she whispered to me, "Mommy, a tear just fell out of my eyes."

Her voice was curious. She didn't know why she was crying. I looked over and saw a few single tears streaming down her cheeks and realized it was the first time she'd cried for someone other than herself. And it was beautiful to watch. Sometimes when our mouths can't find words, our bodies speak for us. At four years old, empathy moved my little girl beyond words and into a language of tears. She didn't know how to explain it and simply whispered, "I like that my tear just talked for me."

The empathetic soul is a brave soul. It is willing to feel emotions, which most people flee from, whether through denial, distraction or down-playing. God is the one who created us with the capacity for emotion. He's who gave us tears to speak for us when our hearts fail, and our words are lost.[90] Emotions are a gift from Him, and they open new chasms to receive His delight.

Emotions help us develop powerful connections, both with others and with God himself. He created us to be feeling creatures, and while we certainly need to keep tabs on what is true or untrue in our emotional state, emotions can serve as a gauge for our life.

Our feelings give us the freedom to be expressive. And when we are expressive, we can pour out love onto others by building them up with encouragement. Yet, for most of my life, I thought my emotions were bad or misplaced or just juvenile.

Everything I thought I knew about emotions changed one day in an airport. I had the perfect layover—just enough time for a black brew from Starbucks and a leisurely perusal through the airport bookstore. I came across a rack of books on emotional intelligence. Shocked to see the words "emotional" and "intelligence" aligned this way, I immediately bought the book.

Prior to that moment, I had spent years suppressing my emotions. I had been taught that emotions were bad and a sign of weakness. I knew I was more emotional than I was *supposed to* be, and I thought that was the end. It seemed too good to be true, to think that what had previously filled me with shame could a good thing, like intelligence.

As I began reading my new book, I learned about emotions through a new lens. I discovered that emotions can be both spontaneous and planned. Emotions can sweep up and surprise us, or they can be emotional states we decide to create for ourselves. The unplanned ones are what most of us think of when we think of emotions. Something bad happens, and we feel sadness. Our boss put pressure on us at work, and we feel stressed out. We don't get a job we had been hoping for, and we feel rejected and discouraged.

But we rarely think about the spectrum of emotions we *can* control and *can* choose. We curate these emotions through our thoughts. Our thoughts drive our feelings, not the other way around. We can trace every feeling back first to an initial thought, so if we focus on our thoughts from the get-go, then we can better understand, manage, and work through the feelings that result.

Cultivating emotions through intentional thought is actually Biblical. In the New Testament alone we are told to "rejoice" 759 times. This is a command, which shows that we have the choice whether to engage in it.

We are the boss of our emotions because we have power over our thoughts. That doesn't mean that unwanted emotions won't sweep into our hearts, suggesting that we bow down to them. They will. They will press in, disrupt and distract us—but they don't get the final say. Emotions can pass, and they can be suggestions we choose not to take. That doesn't mean we ignore them. We must honor them and walk through the full beginning, middle, and end of the emotion. But we don't have to let the emotion determine the state of our heart. We get to decide which emotions we invite to stay awhile, and which ones need to be sent swiftly on their way.

The thoughts you focus on are the thoughts that set your planned emotional state. A positive emotional state comes from positive and intentional thoughts. We can rejoice, no matter the circumstances, because we can first choose in our thoughts to rejoice. The decision of what to think about is like setting the thermostat in a room—it sets the temperature for the entire environment, and in this case, for the feelings you will experience throughout the day.

In order to rejoice, as commanded by verse[91] after verse[92] in the Bible, we have to practice stepping into delight. We have to allow ourselves to feel, to connect, to notice, and to take pleasure in the love that makes up our lives.[93]

Delight is relational. As we rejoice, or delight in—that is, take great pleasure in—the Lord, He also delights in us. But note that this is not a chicken-or-the-egg scenario. Delight always starts with God delighting first in us. We can then respond to His delight with our own delight, simply because He first loved us.[94] Delight multiplies, purely because of its nature.

The more we take pleasure in God, we more we will feel the pleasure that God takes in us. Pleasure, however experienced, turns the mundane into the magnificent. In this place of pleasure, the peace of God can feel tangible. It feels pure, like a wave of innocent joy that washes over your spirit.

Delight delivers freedom. And that freedom can feel dangerous. It's risky. It takes courage to allow yourself to explore emotions you don't yet know or understand well and doing so can feel daunting and intimidating. It feels like opening Pandora's box, where anything could pop out. But in order to get access to the beautiful, life-giving, delight-inducing emotions, we must first be willing to sort through the hurtful, painful, hard-to-express emotions.

I avoided facing the full range of my emotions for years. I didn't think I could handle the negative ones, so I ran from them, covered them up, and pressed them down. They felt too big and like too much. It was all too messy to figure out on my own.

We don't have to do it on our own, though. That's the beautiful thing about being a child of God. He gets involved—close and present—like any parent would do for their child who needs help. When invited in, He never leaves us, even when stuff gets sticky and icky. He waits with us, grieves with us, shelters us, and heals us as we bravely open our hearts to Him to process what we've been avoiding or burying. God specializes in this type of heart work, taking broken, half-engaged hearts and making them fully alive.

I trudged through most of my life half-heartedly. You would have never guessed it, as I hid behind my optimistic and energetic personality, but my heart felt dull. I carried with me a self-consciousness that I just couldn't quite shake. I didn't believe that God was really interested in helping me. When I felt His goodness, I doubted its sustainability—a result of my belief that I wasn't deserving of being loved so deeply.

Understanding the love I have for my kids has helped me understand God's love for me in a different light. When I look at my daughter, I only see Ellie. I don't see her hair color, the

Cheeto dust on her face, or the wispy hairs that run wild. None of those things matter when I think of her, because frankly they have nothing to do with who she is. And it is who she is that matters to me. My heart never changes; I love her for her.

God's love for us is not very different from this. It's just better.

I do my best to love my children well. But, as a flawed human, I have breakdowns. I crumble in frustration. My patience falters. Some days seem impossibly long, and I tire of folding the self-replicating laundry pile. Yet, despite my failings, I still would do anything to let my children know how intimately and unconditionally loved they are.

How much more perfectly does God love us? He knit us together, each so uniquely and intricately.[95] He knew our names at the beginning of time and planned for us to be born at the exact moment in the world's history that we were. He created us and He delights in us, just as we are.

When we shut down our emotions, we disconnect from our Creator. We focus our energy on fixing ourselves, trying to make ourselves loveable again, and avoiding the feelings that get us labeled "too much." The more we feel unsettled in ourselves, the more insecure we feel, the more the discontentment rises within our spirits—and the less we can feel the love of the Father.

Emotions, in whatever way you feel and express them, are powerful. You don't have to identify with being sensitive to need to pay attention to your emotions. Every personality type has a different natural interaction with their emotional side, and we all have the opportunity to use our emotions for deeper connection. To connect in this way, we need to pause and reflect on past powerful emotions, noticing why they happened and how we felt in relationship to others as a result.

Think about the last time you really got excited. I mean, you really got glorious news, or your favorite sports team won a giant championship. I'm talking about the jump-up-and-down kind of celebration, the kind that you can't contain, the kind that overflows joy in such a capacity that it practically becomes tangible.

When my kids were teeny toddlers, our hockey team, the Washington Capitals won the Stanley Cup. It was a nail-biting victory and turnaround story, and it all went down into the wee hours of the night. It didn't matter that it was almost 1AM. We ran upstairs to wake our sleeping children. They needed to experience history; they needed to get to take part in our euphoric celebration as we won. We simply couldn't help it. When the spirit of celebration is in our hearts, we can't help but want to invite others into how we feel.

Christ didn't just come to save us a spot in heaven, He came to give us life *here,* and life to the fullest.[96] And that is something to celebrate. Like, jump up-and-down-celebrate, and wake-up-others-up-celebrate. We do that by giving ourselves permission to be fully alive.

Coming alive comes with a risk. There's so much on the line. Your heart is on your sleeve. You go all in. You love without abandon. You dare to dream. And you do it all in a way that others can see, regardless of what they may or may not think about you.

The beautiful thing is that when you come alive, you show others that they can too.

Think for a moment when you felt whole and wrapped up in beauty. Maybe you were gazing out over the ocean at sunset, entangled in a warm hug or running down a hill with your kids—whatever it was, your soul probably felt like it was erupting with life. Find those moments. Seek them out, stay in them and soak them in with gratitude. They are small ways that we can actively live life to the fullest. You'll know you're doing it—that is, life alive—when you feel this combination of peaceful euphoria, belonging and bliss. It's what you'll feel when you embrace the unknown adventure that God has planned for you here on Earth.

I want to live in such a way that my life cries out with joy, and my life explodes with evidence of its overflow. I'm talking about the joy that makes you want to dance in public. The type of smile so wide and authentic that it is contagious and inviting to all who see it. The type of voice that speaks goodness, faith, hope and encouragement out to this world, to all whose ear hears in a way that genuinely mobilizes change.

I can't change the world on my own. I can only change it through the light that is within me. And for that light to glow, or even dimly on my off days I've got to step into the dark.

For years I wrote myself off as being too emotional to live fully as myself and, as a result, I distanced myself from the One who made me this way. Just like I did as a child pouring all my emotional energy into sports, as an adult I hid my emotional nature by throwing myself into my work. I was ashamed of who I was, constantly on high alert to keep anyone from getting to know the real me. As a result, I felt alone and disconnected from everyone. I felt cursed.

What I didn't know is that self-consciousness and a lack of self-acceptance is not just a curse; it is part of *the* curse. The original curse that happened in the Garden of Eden when Eve ate the forbidden fruit.[97] It's a curse of separation and shame. It removes us from full acceptance; it prevents us from being fully known or fully loved. Self-consciousness drives the concept of conditional love deep into our hearts. If only we can keep being good, then we will be loved. If only we can stay skinny, then we will be loved. If only we can stay pretty, then we can be loved.

You can find conditional love anywhere. It is in abundant supply in our world because it is cheap. It is the love that comes with social media likes, outward affirmations, social status, financial success, beauty, and popularity. And we're drawn to it—I know I am—foolishly chasing it even though we know that it won't last once we get it. It always leaves us thirsty for more.

This thirst is universal. It's a thirst for love and meaning, and the only thing that can fill it is Jesus. He tells us that when we drink from Him, we will never thirst again.[98] Jesus connects us and provides the way for us to be in relationship with God. And it is in God that we find and experience ultimate love: unconditional, unquenchable, unmeasurable love. There simply is nothing we can do to make God love us more[99] In the same way, there is nothing we can do to make God love us less.

Growing up in church, I knew this, but I didn't really believe it. I felt too weird, too on the outside, too misunderstood, and too sensitive—not like the other kids, though I tried hard to blend in. God's pure love for me made little sense. I pushed away my emotions and thought my sensitivity made me defective.

The day I discovered that my emotions weren't a handicap changed everything for me.

It started with that book in the airport, and then the more of the Bible I read, the more I came to understand that God's Word is filled with emotions. God gave us emotions for a reason, and what a gift that we can feel connection to Him because of them.

Emotions are gateways to connection with God; they communicate for us the things that we can't speak—and delight is one such a thing. Those brave saints who allow themselves to be vulnerable are those who experience the greatest measure of tangible delight. So, let's feel our feelings and be fully ourselves, knowing that our emotions are a part of us that God created, a part of us that helps us relate to Him more deeply. You are not too much, and God loves you just the way He made you.

CHAPTER 10

Discovering Delight in Being Present

I f you haven't recently spent time with a two-year-old at the beach, it's a beautiful disaster. It takes tremendous preparation and effort, all to sit, then stand, then sit, then stand, and then de-sand after an hour or two of whining. It's the ultimate example of doing a lot but going nowhere.

The entire aim is to tire your child out, while also keeping them alive and not getting fried by the sun. This is a delicate mission because of the nap schedule, so the best time of the day for this is midday, which is coincidentally the hottest part of the day.

You can forget getting a free minute to sit down and relax under the shade of an umbrella. An eternal optimist, I still always bring a book, a magazine, and a journal with me. *Just in case,* I tell myself. But truth is, with a two-year-old, you move the *entire* time.

Gone are my days of pensive thought while looking out over the ocean and leisurely reading while tanning. I've had to hit a pause on romantic mid-day strolls down the beach with my husband, and I can't as easily partake in pickup games of frisbee or beach soccer. Instead, I get a different exercise. It's a different beach experience we like to call "toddler following."

My little guy has a system for time spent at the beach. First, he runs full speed toward the ocean. Then without slowing down, he belly flops into a crashing wave, sometimes to pick himself back up, and other times to be tossed around in the surf, needing rescue, since he can't swim yet.

Clean and wet, he likes to run back up the beach back to our stuff, grab his toy truck, and push it full-speed towards any neighboring beachgoer peacefully reading a book. Inevitably he trips on his own feet, tumbles, and cakes himself with sand, only to pop back up and change whatever route he was taking.

He garners smiles from spectating sunbathers as he pushes his truck at full speed toward anyone building sandcastles. Seeing a target, the truck gets abandoned, and Baker becomes a Godzilla-like monster, ready to destroy the delicate masterpieces. I have to sprint ahead of him to block the way.

Crisis averted; I redirect him back to his beloved truck. He pushes the truck for ten minutes, and then the cycle starts over. He yells out "boat" or "airplane" to anyone passing by and stops to show his truck to the constant flow of beach walkers at the edge of the water where he plays.

Baker's truck captures his heart.

When he's not knocking down sandcastles, it has his full attention.

Unless a sandpiper, the adorable little shorebird that wades at the edge of the waves shows up. When those little birds arrive on scene, everything gets abandoned, and Baker chases them.

The way he runs after them differs from the way he runs after anything else. When he chases birds, he runs with delight. The smile on his face is simultaneously curious and elated, confidently convinced that he will catch said little sandpiper.

He obviously never does, but that boy never stops trying. He doesn't seem bothered by this. Instead, when the bird flies away, he stops dead in his tracks and looks up to the sky. He reaches out his hand, calling after the birdie to come back, and then happily turns his attention to chasing the next bird.

My son's unwavering enthusiasm for chasing birds is marvelous to watch. In spectating, I lose myself in his delight. Magical and innocent, it transports me back to a place of my childhood. A wave of peace envelops my heart, and through merely watching my son, I am tired but also filled with his delight.

Delight is contagious. And his detachment from the outcome magnifies Baker's delight. This chasing of the sandpipers shows me that we are wired to be in the present, separate from the success we hope for.

Most of my life, I believed the lie that the delight my soul craves comes from arriving at a destination or an accomplishment. Even though I know better, I often focus too much on the finish line rather than celebrating the life-giving journey.

Baker's love for sandpipers reminds me to be different in my approach. He inspires me to return to the innocence of being as present and engaged in the moment. I often get so focused on what I want, on where I hope to go, and on how I want to grow that I miss out entirely on being present. This isn't intentional. I just rarely think I have the time or luxury to

135

slow down—or to run and chase the sandpipers or do anything impractical—until I've gotten "further along." Unlike my son's fruitless pursuit of birds on a beach, I forget that success is not a certain outcome of my actions. Instead, success is finding delight by giving each step along the way my full attention.

My struggle to stay in the moment does not surprise God. He knows we will be impatient and focused on the wrong things, which is why the Bible is packed with counsel to wait and be patient. Be still.[100] Wait on the Lord.[101] Be patient and constant in prayer.[102] Do not grow weary.[103] Have hope and patience.[104] The list goes on and on.

This world makes us restless. We chase happiness like it eludes us, promising ourselves that we will feel happy when we "get there." "There" being when we lose ten more pounds, when we have three months of an emergency fund saved up, or even perhaps when we have just five more comments on a social media post. The world has sold us a lie that once we're "there," we will know it and it will finally be enough.

But what if we're already "there?"

The Bible says that when we return to God—when we believe in Him and trust Him and focus on what He's doing in our lives right now instead of what we want to accomplish in the future—we will be crowned with everlasting joy and be filled with gladness.[105] We don't have to wait until we cross a certain number of tasks off our list or reach a certain level of achievement; we don't have to wait to delight in the beauty and blessings of this world until we "get there." We can start right now.

When I realized I wanted to break free of my obsession with the destination and become more like my son, delighting in the journey, I started with my love of picnics.

Picnics are not a destination; they are an experience. I thought if I could picnic well, and be fully present, then perhaps I could find more ways to do this in my life. This realization showed me that, with God's help, I could shift my perspective, slow down, and relax. Picnics gave me hope.

Like any journey, going on a picnic involves a degree of unpredictability. Picnics are filled with unknowns: Will it rain? Will we accidentally put our blanket on an anthill? Will we be hot and uncomfortable? Will we have packed enough food? The variable nature of picnics guarantees a fresh experience every time. Each picnic is unique and has its own rewards that promise to be unlocked in the experience.

As a kid I had three dreams: to be famous (preferably by being an Olympian), to be pretty (by looking like Rapunzel), and to be happy (by having lots of picnics with people who I loved and who loved me). It all made sense and was my perfect plan. We've already covered how the Olympic dreams turned out. Ironically, my dreams of looking like Rapunzel were dashed when I had the idea of getting a pixie cut to look like my swimming hero, Olympian Janet Evans. With the Olympics and Rapunzel fantasies out of the realm of possibilities, picnics seemed like my only attainable dream.

A lifetime of picnics prepared me for a lesson in living in the moment. I remember a picnic in Santorini, Greece overlooking the water during sunset. Thinking about a picnic with my parents at the pumpkin patch always makes me smile. And I'll never forget all the picnics I've taken with my husband, from blankets unfurled between vines during our dating days to that incredible picnic in Paris when he proposed. Picnics have been one unhurried part of my frequently busy, distracted life.

Jesus came to give us life to the full,[106] not the busy or the successful (by the world's standards). Before my study of Baker's beach runs and the lessons I could learn from picnics, I constantly chased moving finish lines I thought would give my life meaning. I thought a full life meant one filled with accomplishment, achievement, and acceptance by others. And to get that, I had to get busy.

But that's not what God wants for us, His daughters. It has taken some years and resistance, on my part, but I am slowly learning. It's difficult when you are awakened to ugliness in your heart. And for me, this was ugly. I wasn't just addicted to busyness; I worshipped it.

It's not pretty to admit you've had other gods in your life. To be truthful, it's not something I ever thought I would even confess or write. But it's true. I bowed down daily at the altar of productivity.

Productivity is seductive, enticing me away from freedom and contentment with promises of future satisfaction if I just do more, get better, try harder. Productivity gives me a high through an illusion of control. When I put my trust in productivity—what I can accomplish on my own—I replace my faith in God with faith in myself. The problem for me is that I like to do things and to prove myself. I have an addiction to doing. My name is Trish Blackwell, and I am an addict.

Real life doesn't happen when we cross things off our to-do lists, though. It happens when we measure the fullness of our lives by how well we love God and love others. It happens when we have the freedom to play. It happens when we stop doing and start feeling. Real life thrives when we are enough by being ourselves instead of feeling the pressure to prove ourselves.

God cares about who we are, not about what we can do. I see this in how David tells us in the Psalms that God delights in the details of our days.[107] If the God who spoke everything into existence also cares about the details of my day, then surely, I can let go of the reins of control I cling to and let Him care for me.

A clean house, an emptied email inbox, a week's worth of prepped meals or social media posts—this proof of productivity feels good. But what feels *better* is rest and delighting in the presence of the Lord. With God, being present and slowing down isn't a privilege—it's not something to be earned or justified. It is a right, a command, and a generous invitation.[108] Really, it's a gift.

We hold this gift in our hands, but most of the time we don't unwrap it or open it. The gift is abundant life, a rich and satisfying life.[109] But because it doesn't look how we expect, we often keep it wrapped, convincing ourselves that we're too busy to indulge in slowing down and enjoying it. As C. S. Lewis famously wrote, we are "like an ignorant child who wants to go on making mud pies in a slum because he cannot imagine what is meant by the offer of a holiday at the sea. We are far too easily pleased".[110]

Back to picnics and how they've helped me learn to slow down, open the gift of abundant life, and truly live. I'm not the only picnic lover in my family. Each Mother's Day, a group of forty of us drive up to 100 miles to gather in the mountains of Virginia. Our picnic potluck celebrating motherhood has become a cherished tradition—and the best part? Because we are honoring the mothers, we relinquish any mother in our group of all responsibility for the day. This abdication of duty gives us permission to be delightfully irresponsible. The men are in charge of the children and the food, and we spread ourselves out in fields of the rolling Virginia or Maryland countryside, the Blueridge Mountains as a backdrop. Wedges on feet and wine in hand, we teeter like little girls, delighting in the sunshine and beauty.

There's no plan for the day, and nothing productive comes from it—which is perhaps why this is one of my favorite days of the year. You never know what's going to happen at our Mother's Day picnic, so we just show up and enjoy, with no expectations or responsibilities. It's a day in which I feel deep, sparkling delight.

This year the weather seemed to plot against us. My family and I piled into our Jeep, dog in tow, and drove to Maryland in what quickly became a torrential downpour. We couldn't turn around, though, because we knew everyone else was on their way. No one wants to be the one who doesn't show up because of a little of rain. It turns out that "little rain" turned into a lot of rain that lasted almost the entire day.

Once we arrived at the winery, a converted farm property in the foothills of the mountains, the weather continued with a consistent showering of rain. Our party squished into a corner of a small building and the children overflowed out onto the property, which was covered in barns and various awnings intended for pic-nickers on a nice day. It wasn't ideal, but it worked.

The two youngest cousins, one of which was my little Baker, were just eighteen months old. Staying inside a stuffy, overcrowded room with no space to play was not in the books for them, so they squeezed themselves out a door and scooted outside to run. In bow ties and boots they ran circles around each other, jumping in and falling face first into puddles of mud that could have passed for small ponds.

Watching them, I smiled at the fact that once again I was being taught how to live by a little boy less than two years old. Without fail, he challenges me to focus on what can be experienced, not on what can be accomplished. Play is purposeful and powerful. It is not time wasted; it is life gained.

We spent the next hour running in muddy fields, dancing in a leaky barn, and throwing stones to splash mud. I gave no thought to the two-hour car ride home, or that we hadn't brought a proper change of clothes. And when we got to that car ride back? Yes, we were dirty. And yes, the car smelled like stale mud and sweat. But the joy of the day overruled any inconvenience I felt, and all I remember is that we drove through the rolling hills with shared smiles and the satisfaction of a day well lived.

Slowing down and giving ourselves permission to live fully in the moment helps us appreciate what we have. And the joy and connection we get when we do makes it clear what truly matters.

Productivity doesn't matter. No one cares about how much you can achieve or get done. It just doesn't matter. No one cares about your weight, your popularity, your bank account, your job title, your clean house, your social media followers, your success, or whatever measuring stick you are using to give yourself value. What matters is how we loved—and how we were loved by the Lord, the one offering abundant life, life to the full.

Will you let yourself jump in the mud, even if it's unplanned and makes the rest of the day a little messy? Will you take a risk and spend a day unscripted, unplanned, and care-free, with a crown of joy on your head?

For me, this hasn't been easy. But we have good examples to follow. Kids make the best teachers for this. They, more than anyone, know how to be present. It's humbling how they can help us unlearn what we once learned. And since we were all once children, we can relate. We knew their secrets; we saw through their eyes. At one time we were fully present and fully alive. We knew how to delight in life and, even if we didn't have the words for it, to feel God's delight in us.

It's no wonder that Jesus tells us to become like children,[111] for within their perspective and their priorities lies the promise of peace. Kids know what matters. Keep it simple and you will too. When you do, you will thrive—and you will feel the love of God.

The more detached we can make ourselves from the outcome of our efforts, the more joy we will have. It is the journey—in being present—that we get to swim in the life-giving flow of God's abundant peace.[112]

I am like a firefly to light, drawn to the checklists of this world. They pull me in and burn me up. And while you and I might have different struggles, we live in the same world that vies for our attention and affection. The good news is that we do not have to copy the behavior of this world, unless we want to,[113] so the question becomes: How do you want to live?

I have decided that I want to live differently than I have in the past.

I will let go of my to-do list and run with abandon, slowing down to take in the sacredness of life—even if I have to force myself. I will rebel against my desire to bow before the altar of productivity, prestige, and income. I will choose to be different and remind myself every day to keep being different. I invite you to do the same. When we do this, we get to walk through life at a different pace than most. We get to walk a path of peace and purpose instead of the one of chaos and anxiety that paves most of the world.

When we slow down and settle in, we get to relive the freedom of childhood and walk hand in hand with the God of heavens and earth.[114] Holding God's hand makes it easier to trust His good and perfect plan for us—both the big plan for our life and the detailed plan of that mundane, nondescript day.

Let's go chase some sandpipers and roll in the mud, shall we?

CHAPTER 11

Discovering Delight in Being

I can still see my reflection. I was about nine years old, and we were driving down I-95 in our red minivan. I can't remember where we were going or who else was in the car aside from my mother who was driving, but I remember everything else. I was on the left side of the back seat and we were headed south. The sun was shining in just the right way that my body was reflected in the window back to me. And it alarmed me.

I didn't recognize it. I didn't like it.

There were shapes growing where they weren't before. Though I had eagerly waited for what felt like years to become a woman, I didn't like what was happening now that it was happening. It didn't look how I expected or how I thought it was supposed to. I knew God loved me, and that He designed me, but why did He design the other girls my age to look better than me? Why did He create a body so awkward and ill-fitting compared to everyone else? Of course, no one knew this was all going on in my head, but I became convinced I was a mistake.

What I saw in the car window that day looked uncomfortable, wide, and slouched. It was the reflection of a body that looked like it didn't belong where it was. My shoulders seemed too big, and they slumped forward to hide my growing chest. I looked awkward. And for the first time that I can recall, I felt deep shame. I felt ugly. But rather than tell anyone, I internalized my disappointment and kept quiet the rest of the ride.

As we drove along, I began thinking, "If I don't look the way I want to, then I will stand out in other ways. I'll be more by doing more. I'll matter because I'll do things." It was that moment that planted the seed of performance in my little heart. That seed grew deep roots and bore fruit of achievement that rotted as quickly as it ripened. The achievements that decorated my life lost their allure almost as quickly as I reached the milestone. I constantly felt empty and behind.

As I grew older, I convinced myself that I would experience satisfaction as soon as I reached the next level of whatever I was pursuing. First it was athletic achievement, then it was weight loss, then it was social acceptance, then it was climbing the corporate ladder, then it was financial gain and possessions. The harder I tried to feel worthy, though, the more inadequate I felt. Just like that first car window reflection, my distorted image of myself always led to shame. The more I served the gods of affirmation, ambition, and accumulation, the more I felt I was lacking.

I knew I was self-conscious, but I never questioned what my self-consciousness meant. I simply accepted it as part of life as I aged through adolescence. I didn't tell anyone about it. The outside world had the impression that I was smart, athletic, and happy. I was supposed to be happy, so that's what I pretended to be. But in my soul, in the places where it mattered, I was in a constant state of depression and despondency. In some ways, I used the tension I secretly lived in as a justification for some of my private destructive behavior—not that I acknowledged it was destructive.

I wasn't being self-destructive. I was just hard on myself because I had high standards.

I wasn't being weird about my food and exercise. I was just conscious of my body, and my body was flawed, so I needed to do things that other people didn't need to.

I wasn't a workaholic. I was just passionate about making sure I made my mark and that I mattered in this world.

I wasn't comparing myself to others on purpose. I was just someone with social anxiety and insecurity issues and I just couldn't help it.

Excuses. Justifications. Cop outs.

I accepted these underlying feelings as a permanent part of my life. They weren't going away on their own, so I resigned to making do with them. As their roots deepened, being reinforced each year as I aged, I believed that this was just the way it was. I felt cursed and if I'm honest, just a little crazy. This overwhelming self-consciousness convinced me I was not enough, that I was behind, and that, no matter how hard I hustled, I wouldn't measure up or catch a break.

I thought my mind was broken.

The amount of self-consciousness I felt made me feel even more different than I already felt from everyone else. I convinced myself I was alone in my struggle and the self-consciousness intensified. I was certain I was an oddball, and the only one struggling with thoughts about myself.

The self-consciousness we feel isn't the lack we so intimately identify with, but it is part of being in a state of separation—the separation that began when Adam and Eve were forced to leave the garden. Self-consciousness is the feeling we have when we don't know if we belong or where we fit. And we were created to belong.

But here's the good news. I was not cursed. You are not either.

We are living in a curse that the entire world feels. So, if the displacement you feel makes you groan sometimes, then be encouraged: you are not weird. You are not broken. You are not as awkward or misfit as you might think you are. You simply need Jesus. He takes the curse away.[115]

Self-consciousness is the key that opens the gates of shame, telling us we don't belong, convincing us to hide, encouraging us to change who we are so we can be worthy of being loved. It compounds upon itself, minor incident by minor incident, until we internalize a message that we were never meant to believe in the first place—that God messed up when He made us. Eventually, we look elsewhere for meaning and belonging, chasing affirmation and acceptance based on what we do, what we can accomplish, and what we achieve.

I became a poster child of this swirling spiral of overachieving. On the surface, this served me well. I ticked off accomplishments as quickly as I could set goals. Beneath the surface, however, was a different story. I was riddled with anxiety, surviving an unsustainable schedule with coffee and energy.

Broken beliefs create broken systems, and I lived in

both for years. This approach became unsustainable when I became a mother, though. I knew that what I wanted was unrealistic: to be both a full-time homemaker and a full-time entrepreneur. Against my better judgment, I leaned into this "holy hustle" for years, taking pride in how I burned the candle at both ends. As long as my bank account kept growing and I could take my daughter to the library, take hikes, and have playdates during the day, then I kept at my crazy pace. Two years went by while I sacrificed sleep, my marriage, and my joy at the altar of productivity and parenting. I was sleepwalking through life.

My second child's birth rescued me from the pit I didn't even know I was in. Premature, with a traumatic birth story that almost killed us both, his arrival brought me face to face with the value of life. Time in the NICU, days set aside for hospital appointments, and surgeries put a damper on my previous mompreneur work pace and busy life. It was like God hit the pause button in my life and my heart.

The days with my five-pound preemie were long and uncertain, but it was in their slowness that I tasted the peace of being still more vividly than I had ever before. Holding his fragile little body, a body that could fit in one hand, I felt the fragility of life. Like most premature babies, he had weak lungs. I spent my days literally watching his chest rise and fall, seeing every bone of his rib cage as the skin stretched with the contractions. I delighted in the miracle of his breath and was eager to see his next breath happen. He showed me how I had literally taken the gift of breath for granted.

Perhaps it was a renewed appreciation for breath, my brush against death, or looking at that tiny human I almost lost, but those slow months changed my soul. Whatever it was, the birth of Baker birthed a miracle within me—it was a miracle of perspective change.

I loved Baker for breathing. For being in my arms. For existing. For being.

He couldn't do anything. Quite the opposite. He demanded everything from me. And I loved him all the more for who he was, even without yet knowing him in his full personality. Before I even knew how creative, funny, exuberant, and affectionate he is, I loved him for just *being*.

God feels the same way about you, and about me. He loves us even when we are simply resting, breathing, and living in the quietest way. His love for us is steady, and it is faithful. It is beyond our ability to even comprehend. And you're not just lumped into being loved by Him because you are human. The chance of you being born as you is numerically improbable. Some have estimated it to be 1 in 400 trillion, and some research, like Dr. Ali Binazir's, reveals that it might be closer to a 1 in $10^{2,685,000}$ chance.[116] This only confirms the truth that God has specifically created you,[117] knit you together in your mother's womb,[118] and called you, His child.[119]

Having children has shown me how much God loves me. I love the people in my life for who they *are*, not for what they *do*. I love them the most, not when they're doing something extraordinary, but when they're doing the most ordinary things, and just living alongside me. I love my children when they do impressive things, like when my two-year-old ditched his training wheels and rode his bike like a big kid. Or when my five-year-old got up on skis the first time she tried. I love it when they are well-behaved, when they get good remarks from teachers at school, and when they are kind to worms, moths, and the imaginary fairy that lives in the tree in our backyard. But my love for them is separate from those things.

Take those accomplishments away, and my heart still bursts with pride over my children. The things we do in this life are like splashes of paint, adding color to the story of the adventure of our lives are already telling. They decorate the journey; they are not the journey.

The world tells us to have ambition, and unbridled, that ambition can go from driving us to defining us. It clouds our identity, and we take cues about who we are and what matters from others, throwing ourselves into work, busyness, achievement, and accumulation. We pressure ourselves into a position professionally, socially, and financially—and we end up burdened and anxious, needing to keep up with every next achievement rung ahead of us.

There is an easier, lighter way. It's the way of Jesus. The good news is that we don't have to know how to do it. Jesus himself tells us that He will teach us.[120] He will take our baggage, our stresses, our pressures and give us rest. The pace of Jesus is light, peaceful, and beautiful.

And He invites us to copy Him and learn from Him.

It took me over thirty years to realize that I have been copying the wrong pace of life. It's natural: we are wired to emulate the examples of success we see. I simply got confused about what success was and who to copy.

I have had to unlearn my rush and hustle. Truth be told, I'm still unlearning this, and I was so deep in that it might be a lifelong process. It feels awkward and unnatural, but it is the way of Jesus, and I want His way, even though my way feels more comfortable.

I still sometimes second-guess people's intentions, doubting that I could be loved for who I am rather than what I do. Like you, like us all, I am a work in progression, not in perfection. As I lean into discovering delight in being who I am, in simply being, I find God is sprinkling more and more opportunities for me to lean in and *let myself be loved*.

My mother-in-law Marie often says she misses me. It feels like something she "has" to say. For the first few years of our relationship, I always minimized her sentiments. Assuming she meant my entire family, I would answer back, "We miss you too." Correcting me she would confirm that yes, she misses her son and her grandchildren, but also, she specifically misses me. Marie doesn't miss me because of what I do, or how I look, or how I treat her son. She misses me for me. She has mastered the ability to love people simply for who they are, and this still makes me uncomfortable at times. I have so much to learn about loving well and being loved well.

Trusting that people simply want to be with me, for who I am and not for what I bring to the table, has been harder to wrap my head around than I would like to admit. I have never struggled for friends, but I wrote it off because I put effort into being a good friend. I'm an extrovert. I'm easygoing. I pour energy into making people feel good, encouraged, and accepted. So, even in my closest relationships, I still often felt like I was doing my part to belong. With Marie, though, I had done nothing to warrant acceptance. In my mind, I had done nothing extraordinary to merit being missed. And yet, she missed me.

Being yourself, without effort, without performance, without putting on a front, without worrying what others will think, feels vulnerable. It is how we can actually be seen by others. And when you feel seen and valued, it opens the gates to belonging, being loved, and feeling delight.

Marie loves extraordinarily in very ordinary ways. I want to love in the same way. I want my love to be extravagant in how it sees people for who they really are. I want my love to be distinctly separate from what they do, or what they mean to me. I want them to feel the sweet surprise in the soul when they finally believe that I enjoy being with them simply because of who they are, not because of how they measure up to any standard or anyone else.

Comparing ourselves to others is an easy trap to fall into. I can't remember a time in my childhood when I didn't compare myself to my brother. Ellie and Baker, like most siblings, are no different and are constantly battling for my affection. Recently, on our newly refurbished deck, they competed for my attention. I was soaking up rays of sunlight that were pouring onto my new cushioned furniture, delightfully present in the contentment one feels when in the center beam of a ray of light. The kids tried telling jokes, doing dances, and giving little show-and-tell performances, one after another, desperate to outdo the other. *Look at me, look at me, look at me. No, momma, look at me! Look at me! Look at me!*

They talked over one another, as they pushed to get more and more physically close to me. The volume of the conversation escalated until it felt like the entire house was shaking from screams. Determined, they fought to have the loudest voice and the full attention of my gaze.

When this happens, it doesn't matter that I am on the floor, fully engaged and looking directly at them both. They want more. They grab my face with their hands and hold me close, so I don't miss a word of what they want to say. Most of the time, all they are asking is for me to watch them: *Look at me do this, momma!*

We all want this, don't we? We want to be seen, to be acknowledged, and to be encouraged that what we're doing and who we are is something to be noted.

The thing that my littles don't yet understand is that I have *already* seen everything they can do. I see their incredible potential and I marvel at how they are growing in incredible ways. And while I love to applaud profusely and praise them (after all, I am words of affirmation girl), what I most love is when they are sitting and just being with me. I love *being* around them. It doesn't matter what they're doing or how they look; I just like being in their space and having them in mine.

That afternoon on the deck, like so many others, I didn't really care what they were doing or how outstanding it was. What I cared the most about is that they were with me, and I was with them. My heart was content beyond measure simply to be in their presence.

If I clearly comprehend how this plays out as a parent, why then do I ever question that God wants the same with me? He cares about how I show up and use the talents He has given me, sure. But what He cares most about is that I want to be with Him.

The doer in me still wrestles with the simple offer that comes with being in God's presence. It seems almost too easy, too good to be true; but that is exactly what God's love toward us is: too good to be true.

Every ounce of talent or ability I have dormant within me

was first put there by Him. My potential or performance does not surprise him. He smiles at all efforts, as it glorifies Him, but His love for me does not rely on the outcome of my efforts. He looks at me, not to see what I am doing but to invite me closer to Him. He wants to be with me, and for me to be with Him.

He feels the same about you too.

Sister, we can stop performing. We have divine permission to stop striving. He has never asked us to prove ourselves.[121] We have worth, value, and purpose because the Maker of all things said so when He made us. He likes the us that breathes, that walks, that smiles and that looks back at Him, as a child would look back to their father.

It is true: God really delights in you for simply being you.

CHAPTER 12

Discovering Delight in Grief

My biggest fear as a child was that my mom was going to die. It kept me up at night. It made me anxious and constantly on guard for her safety. I understood that death was an inescapable part of life, but I wanted my mom to be above death. I had nightmares about losing her and I experienced separation anxiety anytime she went anywhere without me.

Because I remember so intimately how I felt about the possibility of her death, I am not surprised by my four-year-old's concern about my death. She can't imagine a life in this world without me, so the obvious solution is that we should be sure to both leave the world together. Ellie doesn't mind if I die, as long as she dies at the same time.

Her most recent suggested solution is to go back into my tummy so she can be with me all the time. And though I enjoyed being pregnant, I'll pass on being pregnant and swollen again. This phase has lasted a while now, and I'm okay with it lasting as long as it needs to, for as she questions death, she is also discovering the goodness of life. I want her to know that I am not afraid of death. I'm neither avoiding it, nor seeking it. I am using my energy to live in what I have now. To live well. To live fully.

The thing is, death isn't something that we talk about openly with our friends. It's not exactly dinner party conversation or a subject that comes up at the lacrosse field while waiting for practice to finish. It also might not be a chapter you expect in a book about the delight that God has in you. But this is an important chapter because death surrounds our lives. We don't talk about death enough.

My friendship with Angi blossomed over a conversation about our future funerals. We were young, backpacking in Europe and merely acquaintances on a train heading for a weekend adventure.

She insisted her funeral would have balloons and sugar cookies with smiling faces, that it would be a party where everyone *had* to be happy. Those were her wishes for her funeral. I wasn't sure what to think. No one I had known ever talked about their funerals before they were on their deathbed. And here I was, drinking wine on a train in my young twenties with a glamorous girl I barely knew who was planning the celebration that would be her funeral.

She was at that moment both the weirdest person I knew and the friend I wanted to have for a lifetime. I still remember seeing the French countryside fly past my window and hearing her words dance in my ears. Angi talked about death in a way no one I had ever met had. It wasn't morbid; it was a celebration and gave fresh eyes to see the life in front of me. Sitting with her on that train, as I accepted the promise of death to come, my life came alive. It felt more precious and more important than ever to live it to the fullest, whatever that meant. I spent the rest of my time in Europe that year trying to figure that out.

The ironic thing about death is that it is both known and mysterious. We know we can't escape it, that it's a universal fate for all humans, and yet, we live in shock at the unpredictability of it. I think death disrupts us because it's one of the few things we can't predict, control, or avoid. It reminds us of our humanity and keeps us humble.

Life changes in the blink of an eye. Things happen that we struggle to wrap our heads around. Tragic loss crushes our hearts, we lose hope when someone close to us betrays us, and we feel the overwhelm of bad news that never ends. But when the unthinkable happens to you, it feels like the world stops. All other things fade away, like a blurred-out background, and your eyes become swollen with weariness.

We aren't able to avoid this type of pain and the ache it brings. But though it's painful, when you look closely you can indeed find delight in the delicate. I do not mean that I rejoice in death, quite the opposite. But the delight I have discovered in death is a rally cry to the preciousness of life itself. Like a quiet whisper from God, it conveys urgency to life, preciousness to it, and it gives us purpose to live well before we are called home. And, in its mysteriousness, it boasts of God's majesty, for His thoughts are truly higher than our thoughts.[122]

On a recent Wednesday morning, I dressed my four-year-old daughter Ellie for school. The morning was the typical flurry of brushing teeth, packing backpacks, but this day was special. It was field trip day.

I couldn't push away a pit I felt in my stomach, so I had a few extra "stranger danger" conversations with Ellie than normal. We held hands in the school parking lot as she skipped toward the building, talking about the farm pigs and the goats that she would see that morning with her teachers and school friends.

A few miles away, my friend Kat was doing the same thing. Her daughter Lucy, Ellie's friend and classmate, equally excited for the field trip too. They were having the same conversations—about strangers, about staying close to the teachers at the farm, and about which animals were going to be the coolest. Lucy was wearing a matching t-shirt to Ellie's, and as usual, they were on pace to be at school drop-off at the same time we were. But Kat and Lucy never made it to school that day.

Less than a mile away, on a residential street in our safe suburban neighborhood, an eighteen-year-old lost control of his car, launched across the median, and crashed head-first into the Subaru that carried Kat and Lucy. It was 7:15 in the morning.

Kat, only 34-years-old, two years younger than me, died on the scene. They rushed Lucy to the hospital with serious, but non-life-threatening injuries.

As I walked out of the school that morning, I scanned the parking lot for Kat's car. She was running late, which was unusual for her, and I smiled thinking about how much fun the girls were going to have that day. After I didn't see her the next morning, they informed me that I wouldn't see her again. Kat didn't know Jesus; her funeral had a faint talk of reincarnation and well wishes. Absent was the promise of eternal life, of hope in heaven, or of purpose.

I still see Lucy when I walk my dog and pass the playground. And when I do, I pause. I give her extra affection, extra time, an extra wave, hoping she might know the world is still kind. It robbed her of a mother, and it is not fair.

And life is not fair, at least not in our human understanding of it. God's ways are higher than ours, and our brains simply do not understand some things.[123] It's hard to imagine finding something good in death. Without being motivated by the morbid, I believe that the unpredictability of our lifespans reflects part of God's plan for us to live with delight.

The day is delicate. Breath is uncertain. We aren't promised anything beyond this moment. And with that all in mind, no matter what we believe about God or what we decide about our faith, the delicacy of human life is an undeniable condition of humanity.

People of all walks of faith, and those in complete denial of faith at all, know that there is great wisdom in the one who is able to find delight in the day. The French call it *joie de vivre,* the Danish *hygge*, the Italian *dolce far niente,* and the Costa Ricans *pura vida.* Cultures around the world have traditions grounded in finding delight in the gift of life.

And so, part of the gift of death is that it gives us a gift of life. It helps us understand that life is delicate, a flower to be loved tenderly and appreciated until it withers.

For me, in a season of life where tragic announcements are clogging my social feed, my tender soul has no other choice but to look for the good. After every death I hear about—of those I knew, and those I didn't—I resolve to make my interactions matter more. I better understand the urgency people have to know about the love of Christ.

Somewhere in my twenties, I started tiptoeing with my opinions. I didn't want to offend people with anything I had to say, and so I just stopped saying things. From politics to religion to philosophical musings, the world of being politically correct seeped deeply into my veins and I became cautious.

I called it cautious, but if I were honest, I was cowering. It felt safe to be in the shadows and an onlooker, and it protected me from being the target of other people's criticism or opinions. Really, it was selfishness.

I like it when my friends tell me good news, like a sale at Lululemon or a happy hour special at a local restaurant. It hurts my heart when a friend withholds good news because they assumed I had already heard about it or that I wouldn't be interested in it. In the same way, we have a moral obligation in our humanity to share good news. I wish I had known this sooner; I wish I could take back the decade of missed conversations I never had, but I can't. I have put in my years of playing it safe; now it's time for me to be brave.

It's time for you to do the same. But, friend, don't worry, you're not alone. I'm choosing the brave thing every day too. I will be brave in my love and open with my heart. I will be generous with my words, and transparent about the hope that Jesus fills me with. I will speak my opinion, even if it isn't popular or goes against public opinion. I have seen too much darkness, cried too many tears, and felt too much pain to keep quiet about the source of my hope anymore.

You don't have to look far to find pain in this world. The pain will not stop on this side of heaven; it will ache and rumble throughout the world and we will groan alongside it. But, just as Jesus acknowledged this hard truth, He also promised that we can take heart, because He has overcome the world.

This world will not last forever, nor our experience in it. More than that, we have a promise from God that can get us through all that we don't understand (which, is almost everything, isn't it?). He will wipe away every tear.[124] And He sees every tear that falls from our eyes. Nothing is too small for Him to care about. The hope this gives me is overwhelming, and I want to share this good news with everyone I can.

Talking about God has become offensive to some people, so we skirt around the truth and speak in generalizations accompanied with apologies. No judgment here; I did it too. But the world just got too hopeless. The tragedies piled up; the heartbreak felt like a dirty cloud over the world. Isolation, loneliness, and loss became too in my face to continue as I was. I had to share the hope I had, the hope that we all need.

In order to be right in my spirit, I had to stand firm, be rooted in the Word of God. Sharing my faith felt awfully uncomfortable at first, and I convinced myself that my friends would turn on me. I didn't want to be teased, didn't want to be too "religious," and didn't want to push people away. It turns out that people leaned in. We live in a world desperate for hope, love, and purpose; we live in a culture desperate to be seen and needing to lean in. So, we must be brave. We must show up with truth and honesty. And we can't put it off any longer. Though it feels like we have all the time in the world, we don't. Time is slipping like sand through our fingers, and if you're anything like me, you still feel twenty years younger than you are.

I got notification of my twentieth high school reunion the other week and I actually believed it was a typo. I literally counted out the years on my fingers to make sure the math was right. No way had it been that long. I wonder if this is a lesson on how quickly the next twenty years will go. As I think about those next twenty years, I want nothing wasted. As a person alive in Christ, someone who has felt the delight of God, it is my duty—our duty—to share it with others.

This can be awkward, yes. I am awkward most of the time, though. If we are honest enough, we're all weird, so why are we pretending we're not? Most of the time, it's scary. I have felt tremendous fear sharing my faith and speaking up for what I believe is right. I worried what people might think of me, I feared I might lose listeners or clients, and mostly I wasn't sure if I could stomach rejection from others who might label me and write me off because of my faith.

And for those times when I have a double dose of awkwardness and fear—when I feel like I've been over-the-top encouraging, just a bit too optimistic and high energy, or perhaps even too Jesus-y, I remember Kat. I think of her and of my other sisters around the world who are waiting for hope, desperate for peace, and longing for meaning, but never having a deep or challenging conversation about the hope we get from Jesus because we were afraid to be awkward or afraid of saying the wrong thing.

I have missed too many opportunities, I've skirted away from too many conversations, and I've watered down my passion too many times because I didn't want to offend people by what I believe. Well, that, and let's be honest, I also just wanted them to like me. I cared too much about what they might think. I didn't talk about Jesus because I didn't want people to judge me, so instead of letting them judge me, I judged them and just kept to myself.

Only one opinion matters, though. And it's that of the Judge who we will all have to stand before to recount how we lived.[125] I will be held responsible for my words and my witness. I will be held accountable for my interactions and for how I represented the hands and feet of Jesus here on earth.

I'm guilty of falling into the blindness of youth, thinking I'll never die. I put off being bold in my faith because I just assumed that I had more time. Maybe you don't struggle with this the way I did. If not, it probably means that you've experienced unexpected loss. Because no matter how you slice it, unexpected loss rocks our understanding of life and death and fairness to the absolute core. It's no wonder that in a year riddled with loss, I am finally waking up.

In just a moment, life can be swept away. It might happen to you in ten years, or ten days, or even ten minutes. Only God knows your time. And while that feels alarming to the core, as children of God we do not have to live in fear. If we live, we are sustained in His love[126] and if we die, we gain access to God's full presence in paradise.[127]

We don't get to have this peace about death until we give our hearts fully to God and accept Christ's offering as a blood sacrifice to make us acceptable to God.[128] I believed in Jesus, and was covered in His grace, but it took me years longer to surrender fully to God—trusting Him with all the details of my life and my future.

The day I said a full "yes" to God felt much like any other day. I spent the morning with my kids, checked my email while they played in the backyard, and multi-tasked at the gym with an audiobook. Stepping in place at a furious pace on the stair climber, the author of the book was describing a year in which she said "yes" to everything. I couldn't shake the thought. It overwhelmed my spirit as I continued to listen.

I argued with myself. What if God asked me to do something crazy? Or, even worse, to change something in my life that I like? What if my yeses turned my life upside down, or if I committed but then broke my promise to God when it just got too hard to do?

Committing to saying yes for an entire year felt like too big of a risk. What if God asked me to do something weird, or stupid, or uncomfortable—like talking about Him? What if my life got boring and pointless because He wanted me to stop doing everything that I loved to do? What if my husband thought I was crazy and stopped loving me because I became too religious?

And as I questioned the character of God—and whether I trusted Him and His hand in my life—that His plans for me are better than my own plans for myself, I had my answer. I wasn't enthusiastic about it, but I knew enough to know not to argue with God about things that are unfathomably bigger than me. So, I said, yes, Lord, I will say yes.

It has been just over a year to the date later since that first "yes," and unsurprisingly this has been the most fulfilling year of my life. The year hasn't been filled with typical big life milestones, like the birth of a child, a change in marital status, or a career change. But in terms of unseen milestones, monumental change has happened. And it happened all in my heart. The peace in my heart doubled, I felt genuine joy in my daily life, and deep purpose settled confidently into my spirit.

I'm learning to delight with extravagance in the smallest and simplest of things, and it's difficult. I used to save up a celebration for "big" things, not "normal" things. But is any moment truly normal?

Brandon and I had been holding onto a bottle of 2011 Velvet Glove Shiraz for seven years. They gave it to us as a wedding gift and it sat on our wine rack prominently, year after year, untouchable. When a bottle is beautiful, it's one thing. This bottle was better than beautiful. A deep chocolate black, it was covered in soft velvet and then packaged in a large, expensive-looking box also lined in midnight velvet. It is a wine to be saved for an occasion that really mattered. And so, we waited and waited.

I want to live in a way that doesn't put off celebration, but this bottle was a mirror showing me my hypocrisy. I didn't want to keep holding onto it, but it pulled on me—the longer I held onto it, the more I wanted the time we uncorked it to be magical and memorable. I wanted the moment to matter, and so I decided that important moment would be when I became a New York Times bestseller—the ambitious dream of every writer.

Then, during the quarantine of 2020, in the days of mundane repetition and isolation, we opened the bottle. I resisted this idea at first, because sometimes I get an unexpected stubborn flare and lack flexibility. Loss was dominating our lives, so instead of celebrating an achievement, we decided it mattered more to celebrate the gift of life.

It was a rainy Saturday night and our kids had spent the afternoon vacillating between fighting and playing, screaming and giggling, being adorable and being put into time-out. My heart was heavy—with the weight of the news of the world, the talk of coming famine in third-world countries, and the rising death toll from the virus. These announcements flooded my world with every news notification ping that woke up my phone and iPad throughout the day.

It's easy to look at statistics, numbers, and predictions without emotion, but when we slow down and give ourselves the space to think, the callous layers of protection shed, and we ache. Every number is a name, every name has a story, and every story matters. That week there was one new name added to the count that mattered in particular to me: Amy.

Amy was my age. And just like that, she was gone. Her fight against cancer was graceful, like a tapestry of goodness that flowed from her soul. She never complained, she never speculated, she never openly feared for her young son, and she never felt sorry for herself. She just walked the path that was put before her, changing her gait as the path got rockier and rockier. Eventually, the path led her to the arms of Jesus and away from all pain.

The week prior she and I had been texting, business as usual. She was healthy. She had good days and bad days, but she said she was doing well. We were planning a play date for our kids—and a wine date for us. And then, in the blink of an eye, she was gone.

We had been next-door neighbors for over two years, sharing a wall between our townhomes. More than possibly anyone I have ever known, Amy's life intertwined with ours in a rhythm of slowness, simplicity, and sharing. We shared tools, toys, tacos, and turns taking care of each other's dogs. We spent Saturday afternoons sitting on lawn chairs in her driveway, watching our kids tire themselves out. We wrapped Christmas presents together, did pizza and movie nights in each other's houses, and set up extra egg hunts for the kids at Easter. When it rained, we stood huddled under umbrellas together and let the kids jump in puddles. We lived and did life, side by side, in everyday moments that now seem extraordinary.

For that reason, on an ordinary night, my husband and I opened that $200 bottle we had been saving. I had wanted to drink it on the deck with lights lit and music playing, but it started raining. I had wanted to drink it while the kids were with a sitter, but social distancing meant the only approved babysitter for the season was the television.

There is no reason to save something for a special moment when any moment can be made special. And in that moment, on that night, the memory of our mundane moments together with Amy made them magical.

I'm awful at slowing down, and I'm quick to look past what matters. But when Amy died, I simply couldn't use those bad habits as excuses anymore. Amy shifted something in me, both in her life and her death. And every time I choose delight over delay, and celebration instead of looking for what's next, I feel right. I can feel my heart stir with memories of Amy and the simple lesson of what it really means to live well.

Look, life is delicate. It is fragile. It is of the utmost worth, to be preserved and cherished. It deserves our delight. If you think about it, we care for that which is fragile pretty well. When we move, we pack boxes with the word *fragile* all over them, and we move them with extra caution. When I get an expensive gift, I put it in a special spot. I pay attention to it with more regard—like paying attention to the right moment to drink an expensive bottle of wine.

Fragility makes us pay attention in a good way. It makes us cherish things.

As my heart grieves loss and aches over the uncertainty of life, I choose also to let it rejoice. As I think about Kat, Amy, and my daughter, I taste sweetness. Death will come. I rejoice, though, because I taste the peace of knowing that it is coming. We get to know it is coming and we get to choose what it will mean. We get to know where we will go—to the place where every tear is wiped away and the streets are paved with gold.[129] We win if we live and we win if we die.[130] And while we wait for that moment when we reunite with the King of everything, we get to share our hope with others—and we get to live in such a way that we decide now what people will say about us once we are gone by how we choose to live.

For the moment, and the rest of my moments on this side of Heaven, I am practicing the art of being fully present in the day I have. I have a long way to go in the mastery of this, but I'm reaping the rewards already. And every time my heart grieves at the news of loss, I give thanks for the reminder of the gift of today.

Soak it in and let your heart be glad, for today is the day that the Lord has made, and we get to rejoice and be glad in it.[131]

CHAPTER 13

Discovering Delight in the Taste of Heaven

You've reached the last chapter of the book. I love that feeling, don't you? I get that subtle, yet powerful sense of accomplishment, and I start speed reading to finish the pages. So, go ahead, soak in the feeling of accomplishment you feel. I feel it too. But I urge you, don't rush through these words, for they just might spark something that's been waiting to awaken within you.

Have you ever had a brain freeze from eating ice cream too quickly? Rushing good things takes pleasant experiences and sours them. Ice cream is sweet, and worth savoring—as are the concepts in this book, so let them settle into your soul.

In high school, I juggled three jobs in the summer, one of which was at a local mom-and-pop ice cream shop. Before working at that little shoppe, I had never witnessed happiness so tangibly. And I watched kids play in a pool all day long for a living, so that's saying something. Ice cream differed from play, though—it was indulgent, unnecessary, and just plain extra.

And it should have felt that way—tasting ice cream on a hot day is what makes the summer season. In the smallest of ways, it's a taste of heaven on earth.

I worked at the ice cream shop right after dinner time, typically from 7 p.m. to 11 p.m. Scooping happiness for families was rewarding beyond what I could have ever expected. I considered myself an exceptional employee; however, I probably wasn't the best for the bottom line. It was impossible to not over-serve the eager little children with faces pressed up to the ice cream display. Looking across the counter at them felt like looking at a nostalgic postcard of what summer nights with families are supposed to be. My own memories of ice cream with my grandparents made me even more of a sucker. I couldn't help but give patrons about thirty percent more than what they paid for. I was a crowd favorite.

When business was slow, I made myself an ice cream dinner. It was the kind of thing only an adolescent with a ridiculous metabolism can get away with, and still to this day I don't understand how I didn't get sick.

I would take a full-sized milkshake cup, fill it with rainbow confetti sprinkles, and dab it with vanilla soft serve ice cream—just enough to glue the sprinkles together in sugary conglomerates. Even as I type this, my mouth salivates at the memory of the light, yet ridiculously indulgent taste.

At the time, I was far from living with unbridled joy. In fact, I was deep in the trenches of my eating disorder. But for a moment, those sprinkle dinners gave me a taste of a life that was better than what was currently mine, a life I yearned for. And that is the promise of the gospel. Not that things will be easy, or even objectively better once we walk with Christ—but that we have tastes of joy that give us hope for the future.

Like the dream-come-true dinner made of sprinkles and ice cream, knowing Jesus gives us glimpses of a life sweeter than we can imagine. When we let Him into our hearts, He flips upside down everything we have ever known, or thought is possible. He helps us unlearn what we have learned so we can learn what matters more.

Sometimes this upside-down flip happens internally, and it's ever so slight. Other times, the world, either on a personal level or worldwide spectrum, is flipped over and spilt out over everything. It might be an unexpected loss, a health issue, social complications, an economic recession, a civil war, a war within yourself, or a global pandemic. Unrest will happen. It is an almost guaranteed element of the human experience.

I didn't plan to finish writing this book at the beginning of the outbreak of Covid-19, but here I am, ten days into complete social isolation, with our world turned upside down. No one knows what will happen, expect for you, dear reader, because you are in the future as I write. And just that thought itself gives me hope.

Covid-19 is a halt-stop to the world. People have stopped work. Businesses are closing down. Playgrounds have caution tape or barricades around them. Roads are empty and parking lots of previously busy shopping centers are desolate. There is a government mandate to stay six feet away from all other humans, aside from immediate family members. Schools are closed indefinitely. People are not leaving their houses. We wipe down anything anyone else has touched. There is so much we just don't know or understand. The news tomorrow might change everything—one way or the other—with a vaccine, or with a worse death count than days previously.

I know I will look back at this season with wonder and gratitude, safely reminiscing without the discomfort of the unknown. But the unknown is uncomfortable and upsetting.

In a world obsessed with productivity and accomplishment, slowing down isn't something we do well. Sure, it's talked about and highly recommended by professionals, but typically it stops at that. We have convinced ourselves that we're too busy to do anything other than what we're currently doing to just keep up with our lives.

This virus is stopping life, in a way we have all needed but would have never pursued on our own. In how the sun stood still for Joshua for a full day and never set, allowing Israel to defeat the Amorites,[132] this is society standing still.

Our society—our busy lives in particular—have been stripped down to the bare bone basics. It is unlike anything the world has ever seen. And it happened in the blink of an eye.

I didn't know this was coming, no one could have, but I knew God was nudging me about a change I needed to make in my own life. I knew I was doing too much, and needed to slow down, but I didn't know how, and so I didn't start. A global pandemic forced me to listen.

I had learned a year earlier how to slow down and do less, but life caught up to me, and I fell into old patterns. We had a lot going on—my business was booming, my son was having complex and intensive surgery, my family was grieving some family deaths and medical diagnoses, and we were preparing to move.

Stress had become such a natural part of my life that I didn't even know I was stressed. I knew I felt *off* but convinced myself that I was fine. My life was cluttered and filled to excess.

In our American culture it was all justifiable and normal, but in God's plan it wasn't what He had intended for me.

The coronavirus made me stop. After waffling about how to cut back on the busyness of life, I was shocked to see how quickly it happened when the decision was taken out of my hands, and how easy it was to strip down life to the absolute essentials in order to hide inside our house from the invisible monster of Covid-19. My son has compromised immunity and sensitive lungs, so we were more cautious than others out of necessity. I would do anything to protect my babies, and I did.

The chaos of the pandemic has been a reminder of the unpredictable nature of life. In our modern lives we have created systems to give us a sense of control, but tragedy reminds us how senseless our efforts actually are.

I'm compelled by the uncertainty of it all. In my mid-thirties, I think I am young, but isn't our youth actually relative to how many days we have left to live? And since it's anyone's best guess who will live long and who will die young, I don't know if I am old or young. If God calls me home in my forties, then I'm actually old right now. If I live into my nineties, then I'm still a baby in life, with decades left to live.

These facts make me want to lean all the more into the sweetness of life that's offered. For far too long I have put it off, thinking that I would "earn it" later, have time to indulge in it when I was more accomplished and established, and that I could slow down to savor when I was far enough along. I've been waiting to "arrive" in life.

But we have arrived.

There is nothing more to prove, no one else to impress, no further weight to lose, no amount of money to make. Nothing to change. You and I have arrived because we are loved.

Sister, please remember that the fight for your faith is the most important fight of your life. You are not fighting for your salvation; you have that already, and it is an irrevocable gift. No, you are fighting for a life that brings a taste of Heaven to Earth. It is one of fullness and a life that speaks with healing influence and authority for our fellow sisters. This is not about what I can do, and this is not about what you can do; it is about what we can do together, cheering one another on to watch over our hearts.[133]

We are destined for this. We are the women for the job. We were assigned the good works He has intended us to do in this world before we were even born,[134] and yes, it feels big. And that's why God wanted me to remind you that you are mighty.

The world before us seems big, too big for us. The depression, the abuse, the trafficking, the injustice, the poverty, the addictions, the eating disorders, the perfectionism, the anxiety, the distraction—how will we ever break through the noise, stress, and comparison to offer hope and peace?

We do it by simply lifting our eyes to the hills—to where our help comes from.[135] And as we do, we can smile, for we feel safe and powerful in the love that God has for us. That love makes us secure, and when we are safe like that, we can confidently speak up, no matter how small we might perceive our voice to sound. It is not too small for God to use. When you feel small and when the thing before you seems big, ask God to make up the difference.

We will rise and stand before the giants that taunt and intimidate us. And we will stand firm, even if we feel ill-equipped, exhausted, and overwhelmed. Our light doesn't come from us. The light we shine is merely a reflection of God's love within us, and that love is inexhaustible.[136] We don't have to feel disqualified if we feel inadequate. On the contrary, God does not ask us to be able; He asks us to be available.

If we say, yes Lord, here I am,[137] then He will keep our lamps burning and our light inextinguishable.[138] He will light up our darkness so we can light the way for others. We have all that we need to win against whatever giant we are fighting, for we fight with supernatural power. We have the power of Jesus Christ Himself inside us through our access to the Holy Spirit, and we have God's love surrounding us in protection.

Before he became king, David spent most of his life in obscurity. The youngest of his family, often overlooked and renegaded to a life in the fields, tended sheep. He was small; his father forgot him, and he was the last person anyone would have expected to become the warrior that saved a nation.

David picked up a stone from a riverbed, a source of life— and used it. A small stone from a small boy knocked down and killed a notorious giant that no one else could kill. In the same way, dear sister, you and I pull our weapons from the source. We fight with truth, with hope, with life, with the love of God—and against insurmountable odds, like David, we will be victorious. It is already our birthright.

Thank you. Yes, I am saying it to you. Because I know you are going to pick up a stone to strike. I don't know what your stone looks like, but I know it feels small. Maybe you think it's so insignificant it couldn't really make a difference, but it can, and it will. Your willingness to show up in small ways is a demonstration of your faith in the big ways God will move through you. Remember, we serve a God who delights in taking what is small and doing big things with it—He loves to show off his glory, which He does by taking our little and turning it into something big.

So, from me to you, *thank you*. Thank you for showing up in the world. Thank you for showing up and speaking up for our other sisters who don't yet know how profoundly they are loved.

Your stone might be scrubs, a paintbrush, a keyboard, a muffin pan, or a seat in a PTA meeting in your community. It's whatever is accessible to you right now and in your hands today. It doesn't need to look or sound impressive; it just needs to be picked up and used with purpose. I know you might sometimes look at what you are doing and feel insignificant, so overlook-able, so small, but remember David.

Your weapon might be your words that you write in your blog, it might be your faith in how you remain hopeful in the face of a scary medical diagnosis, it might be little kisses on boo-boos, or the small acts of kindness you consistently do in for your neighbors, the ones who like you and the ones who are more closed off. Do not despise small beginnings[139] or what might feel small, because God excels at taking what is small and doing big things with it. He specializes in using the unassuming, the overlooked, the it-doesn't-make-sense people and things for His glory.

It is in His character; it is part of who He is, and since He is immutable,[140] unable to change who He is, He will do the same for you. He took David's small stones and killed a warrior. He took a snack and multiplied it to feed 20,000.[141] He empowered Gideon, the smallest of his tribe, to defeat an army of 32,000 with just 300 men.[142] He used Esther, an orphan with no influence, to save the Jewish people from annihilation.[143] He used Harriet Tubman, an illiterate slave, to free 300 slaves and change a country. He's using you too. He takes highly unlikely people and creates highly unlikely outcomes.

God likes to use the nobodies of the world. That's you, and that's me. It's us, together. But the beautiful thing is that God's love makes us more than just a somebody. It makes us children of the King, royal, adored and with influence.

Come, sister, out of the shadows and the safety of the believing the lies that you are average or that you have to earn your place in the world or in God's plan. He did not create you to blend in; you are called to stand out. You are a light on the hill,[144] and the world needs you now more than ever.

As you walk and live as light, you bring heaven to earth. Heaven is sweet. And to share its sweetness to others, you must first taste it yourself, which we can do when we spend time in God's Word. His Word is sweeter than honey,[145] more desired and finer than gold,[146] and it gives us refuge.[147] So, make space to taste and see that the Lord is good. Devour the deliciousness of delight He has dripped like heavenly honey into your life. Do this by spending time with Him. Read His Word, live at a pace that allows for quiet in your life, and pay attention to the surrounding goodness. Remember, you are a daughter of the King; you have a direct line and access to the riches of a glorious inheritance.[148]

The more sweetness we taste, the more our praises for His delight will burst forth from our mouths. Our palette for sweetness matures with time. The childhood candy of your past probably doesn't taste as satisfying and deep as your current favorite indulgence. In the same way, our ability to taste the sweetness of God in our lives becomes more refined as we explore it and mature ourselves. God's goodness isn't just sweet; it is decadent, like a seven-layered cake.

I'm an icing girl. I eat cake for the icing, so to me, there is no contest. A seven-layer cake has more icing and, therefore, more richness and beauty to it than just cake itself. In the same way, as your receptors to God's love develop, the sweetness your soul savors will layer upon itself, building up a decadence that overflows and must be shared.

Cake is not meant to be eaten alone. Even cupcakes, which are single serving cakes, get baked in batches of six to twelve. Goodness is only good if there's more than enough of it to go around, and with God's goodness, that's simply its nature.

As a little girl, I fantasized about winning sweepstakes. If there was a public contest, competition or giveaway, I entered enthusiastically, even though I knew the odds were against me. Someone had to win, right? And they did. I followed the stories and romanticized how their lives changed with the windfall of a free bike, a million dollars, a trip to Disney World, or Slurpees for life. The life-time supply prize was always my favorite. I craved the certainty and promise of something good for life that would never be taken away from me.

Here's what I want you to know. You've won the sweepstakes.

It's God's delight. It's both how He feels toward you and how He expresses that around you. Delight is the ultimate lifetime prize. It is cake for breakfast for life. Goodness, for life. Faithfulness, for life. Honey from Heaven, for life.

I am here to wake you. I want my words to stir you from what you have always known. I am here to remind you that you are mighty—and that the world is desperately in need of you to show up. And I know too that without confidence, you won't have courage to step up to the line. Without knowing first that you are deeply loved and intimately known by the creator of the universe. It's true.

And, sister, if it takes a little while for you to believe that to be true in your heart, for you to believe what I am writing, it's okay. This book has a snooze alarm that will continue to remind you it's time to rise. It is your time. It is time to rise and be fully alive.

Straighten your crown, because the King is looking at you with adoration and delight. You have nothing to prove and nothing to lose. You belong, sister. You matter. You have grand purpose. You have everything you need and all that you will ever need. So, stand tall, be yourself, and let the world around you know just how good your Father is.

Acknowledgements

Thank you, first and foremost, to the Lord my God, for allowing me to be a messenger of life and truth to my sisters in this world.

Writing a book is the act of taking an invisible idea and making it something you can hold in your hands. The process is daunting and demanding, and the hours, weeks, and months blend in a beautiful chaos of writing, editing, and re-writing. This book would not have been possible without the support of my husband Brandon and my beautiful children Ellie and Baker. They honored my weekly writing time by bringing me coffee and keeping the house relatively quiet as I worked. They believed in this book even when it took longer to write than expected. They asked me questions and listened to my ideas. They loved me every step of the way.

Thank you also to my parents, Diane and George Blackwell who raised me to have the courage to be myself and the confidence to believe I can do anything I set my mind to. Thank you to my brilliant brother Nick Blackwell, who was always up for chatting about the writing process. Thank you to my mother-in-law Marie Anderson, for allowing me to share some of the early ideas for this book with her and the feedback, wisdom, and prayer she shared back.

My heart has deep gratitude for every listener who is part of *The Confidence Podcast* family, every person who has watched my YouTube Channel and every reader who has read my previous books or my blog. Thank you to my students in *the College of Confidence* and to my clients for allowing me to be a voice of influence and encouragement in their lives. Being your coach and seeing God transform you from the inside out gave my writing in this book more power and confidence. To all the individuals I have had the opportunity to lead and coach, or be led and coached by, I want to say thank you for being an inspiration to much of this work.

To my editorial team, this book wouldn't be what it is without you. Thank you to my editor Mary Carver for smoothing out the rough edges of my writing and improving the book. Thank you to my teammate Anna Barr for your relentless encouragement, your enthusiasm, and your pivotal support in the launch process. Thank you to my book launch coach Massiel Valenzuela, who helped move this book along through every stage from rough draft to final copy. To the women who have been in my life that inspired some of the stories in these chapters, thank you. I wouldn't be who I am without you.

Thank you, dear reader, for allowing me to spend time with you in these pages. I pray that my words will etch confidence in your heart and keep your crown straightened, never forgetting that you are a daughter of the King: beautiful, seen and loved.

Notes

All verses referenced below are in the New Living Version (NLT).

1 Take delight in the LORD, and he will give you your heart's desires. (Psalm 37:4)

2 For the Lord your God is living among you. He is a mighty savior. He will take delight in you with gladness. With his love, he will calm all your fears. He will rejoice over you with joyful songs. (Zephaniah 3:17)

3 For those who are led by the Spirit of God are the children of God. So you have not received a spirit that makes you fearful slaves. Instead, you received God's spirit when he adopted you as his own children. Now we call him, "Abba, Father." For his Spirit joins with our spirit to affirm that we are God's children. And since we are his children, we are his heirs. In fact, together with Christ we are heirs of God's glory. But if we are to share his glory, we must also share his suffering. (Romans 8:14-17)

4 I look up to the mountains – does my help come from there? My helps comes from the Lord, who made heaven and earth! (Psalm 121:1-2)

5 He will feed his flock like a shepherd. He will carry the lambs in his arms, holding them close to his heart. He will gently lead the mother sheep with their young. (Isaiah 40:11)

6 For he will order his angels to protect you wherever you go… When they call on me, and I will answer; I will be with them in trouble. I will rescue and honor them. (Psalm 91:11,15)

7 He replied, "What is impossible for people is possible with God." (Luke 18:27)

8 "If a man has a hundred sheep and one of them wanders away, what will he do? Won't he leave the ninety-nine others on the hills and go out to search for the one that is lost?" (Matthew 18:12)

9 At that time I will hide my face from them on account of all the evil they commit by worshipping other gods. (Deuteronomy 31:18)

10 No power in the sky above or in the earth below—indeed, nothing in all creation will ever be able to separate us from the love of God that is revealed in Christ Jesus our Lord. (Romans 8:39)

11 God showed how much he loved us be sending his one and only Son into the world so that we might have eternal life through him. This is real love—not that we loved God, but that he loved us and sent his Son as a sacrifice to take away our sins. Dear friends, since God loved us that much, we surely ought to love each other. (1 John 4:9-11)

12 What shall we say about such wonderful things as these? If God is for us, who can ever be against us? (Romans 8:31)

13 "I have told you all this so that you may have in me. Here on earth you will have many trials and sorrows. But take heart, because I have overcome the world." (John 16:33)

14 And we know that God causes everything to work together for the good of those who love God and are called according to his purpose for them. (Romans 8:28)

15 "My thoughts are nothing like your thoughts," says the Lord. "And my ways are far beyond anything you could imagine. For just as the heavens are higher than the earth, so my ways are higher than your ways and my thoughts higher than your thoughts." (Isaiah 55:8-9)

16 And who can win this battle against the world? Only those who believe that Jesus is the Son of God." (1 John 5:1)

17 All praise to God, the Father of our Lord Jesus Christ. God is our merciful Father and the source of all comfort. He comforts us in all our troubles so that we can comfort others. When they are troubled, we will be able to give them the same comfort God has given us. For the more we suffer for Christ, the more God will shower us with his comfort through Christ. (2 Corinthians 1:3-5)

18 So if you sinful people know how to give good gifts to your children, how much more will your heavenly Father give good gifts to those who ask him. (Matthew 7:11)

19 The LORD is good, a strong refuge when trouble comes. He is close to those who trust in him. (Nahum 1:7)

20 Be still in the presence of the LORD, and wait patiently for him to act. Don't worry about evil people who prosper or fret about their wicked schemes. (Psalms 36:7)

Your unfailing love is better than life itself; how I praise you! (Psalm 63:3)

21 "So be strong and courageous! Do not be afraid and do not panic before them. For the LORD your God will personally go ahead of you. He will neither fail you nor abandon you. (Deuteronomy 31:6)

22 What is the price of two sparrows—one copper coin? But not a single sparrow can fall to the ground without your Father knowing it. And the very hairs on your head are all numbered. So don't be afraid; you are more valuable to God than a whole flock of sparrows. (Matthew 10:29-31)

The LORD directs the steps of the godly. He delights in every detail of their lives. (Psalm 37:23)

23 But the LORD said to Samuel, "Don't judge by his appearance or height, for I have rejected him. The LORD doesn't see things that way you see them. People judge by outward appearance, but the LORD looks at the heart." (1 Samuel 16:7)

24 "I knew you before I formed you in your mother's womb. Before you were born I set you apart and appointed you as my prophet to the nations." (Jeremiah 1:5)

25 You saw me before I was born. Every day of my life was recorded in your book. Every moment was laid out before a single day had passed. (Psalms 139:16)

26 For we are God's masterpiece. He has created us anew in Christ Jesus, so we can do the good things he planned for us long ago. (Ephesians 2:10)

27 God saved you by his grace when you believed. And you can't take credit for this; it is a gift from God. Salvation is not a reward for the good things we have done, so none of us can boast about it. (Ephesians 2:8-9)

28 Then Christ will make his home in your hearts as you trust in him. Your roots will grow down into God's love and keep you strong. And may you have the power to understand, as all God's people should, how wide, how long, how high, and how deep his love is. May you experience the love of Christ, though it is too great to understand fully. Then you will be made complete with all the fullness of life and power that comes from God. (Ephesians 3:17-19)

29 You will keep in perfect peace all who trust in you, all whose thoughts are fixed on you! (Isaiah 26:3)

30 The thief's purpose is to steal and kill and destroy. My purpose is to give them a rich and satisfying life. (John 10:10)

31 Stay alert! Watch out for your great enemy, the devil. He prowls around like a roaring lion, looking for someone to devour. (1 Peter 5:8)

32 We destroy every proud obstacle that keeps people from knowing God. We capture their rebellious thoughts and teach them to obey Christ. (2 Corinthians 10:5)

33 We destroy every proud obstacle that keeps people from knowing God. We capture their rebellious thoughts and teach them to obey Christ. (2 Corinthians 10:5)

34 "My thoughts are nothing like your thoughts," says the Lord. "And my ways are far beyond anything you could imagine. For just as the heavens are higher than the earth, so my ways are higher than your ways and my thoughts higher than your thoughts. (Isaiah 55:8-9)

35 And we know that God causes everything to work together[a] for the good of those who love God and are called according to his purpose for them. (Romans 8:28)

36 For we are God's masterpiece. He has created us anew in Christ Jesus, so we can do the good things he planned for us long ago. (Ephesians 2:10)

37 Surely your goodness and unfailing love will pursue me all the days of my life, and I will live in the house of the Lord forever. (Psalm 23:6)

38 You will live in joy and peace. The mountains and hills will burst into song, and the trees of the field will clap their hands! (Isaiah 55:12)

39 Anyone who believes in me may come and drink! For the Scriptures declare, 'Rivers of living water will flow from his heart.'" (John 7:38)

40 So their father, Jacob, finally said to them, "If it can't be avoided, then at least do this. Pack your bags with the best products of this land. Take them down to the man as gifts—balm, honey, gum, aromatic resin, pistachio nuts, and almonds. (Genesis 43:11)

41 But Jonathan had not heard his father's command, and he dipped the end of his stick into a piece of honeycomb and ate the honey. After he had eaten it, he felt refreshed. (1 Samuel 14:27)

42 He brought us to this place and gave us this land flowing with milk and honey! (Deuteronomy 26:9)

43 May you experience the love of Christ, though it is too great to understand fully. Then you will be made complete with all the fullness of life and power that comes from God. (Ephesians 3:19)

44 For I will bring them into the land I swore to give their ancestors—a land flowing with milk and honey. There they will become prosperous, eat all the food they want, and become fat. But they will begin to worship other gods; they will despise me and break my covenant. (Deuteronomy 31:20)

45 But the Holy Spirit produces this kind of fruit in our lives: love, joy, peace, patience, kindness, goodness, faithfulness, gentleness, and self-control. There is no law against these things! (Galatians 5:22-23)

46 Then you will experience God's peace, which exceeds anything we can understand. His peace will guard your hearts and minds as you live in Christ Jesus. (Philippians 4:7)

47 The thief's purpose is to steal and kill and destroy. My purpose is to give them a rich and satisfying life. (John 10:10)

48 And it is impossible to please God without faith. Anyone who wants to come to him must believe that God exists and that he rewards those who sincerely seek him. (Hebrews 11:6)

49 For the Lord God is our sun and our shield. He gives us grace and glory. The Lord will withhold no good thing from those who do what is right. (Psalm 84:11)

50 Give your burdens to the Lord, and he will take care of you. He will not permit the godly to slip and fall. (Psalm 55:22)

51 So humble yourselves under the mighty power of God, and at the right time he will lift you up in honor. (1 Peter 5:6)

52 And let the peace that comes from Christ rule in your hearts. For as members of one body you are called to live in peace. And always be thankful. (Colossians 3:15)

53 Make it your goal to live a quiet life, minding your own business and working with your hands, just as we instructed you before. (1 Thessalonians 4:11)

54 Since God chose you to be the holy people he loves, you must clothe yourselves with tenderhearted mercy, kindness, humility, gentleness, and patience. (Colossians 3:12)

55 Don't copy the behavior and customs of this world, but let God transform you into a new person by changing the way you think. Then you will learn to know God's will for you, which is good and pleasing and perfect. (Romans 12:2)

56 Surely your goodness and unfailing love will pursue me all the days of my life, and I will live in the house of the Lord forever. (Psalm 23:6)

57 For I will bring them into the land I swore to give their ancestors—a land flowing with milk and honey. There they will become prosperous, eat all the food they want, and become fat. But they will begin to worship other gods; they will despise me and break my covenant. (Deuteronomy 31:20)

58 So if the Son sets you free, you are truly free. (John 8:36)

59 Give all your worries and cares to God, for he cares about you. (1 Peter 5:17)

60 Then Jesus said, "Come to me, all of you who are weary and carry heavy burdens, and I will give you rest. Take my yoke upon you. Let me teach you, because I am humble and gentle at heart, and you will find rest for your souls. For my yoke is easy to bear, and the burden I give you is light." (Matthew 11:28-30)

61 Give your burdens to the Lord, and he will take care of you. He will not permit the godly to slip and fall. (Psalms 55:22)

62 The Lord says, "I will guide you along the best pathway for your life. I will advise you and watch over you. (Psalm 32:8)

63 And God will generously provide all you need. Then you will always have everything you need and plenty left over to share with others. (2 Corinthians 9:8)

64 For we live by believing and not by seeing. (2 Corinthians 5:7)

65 The Lord says, "I will guide you along the best pathway for your life. I will advise you and watch over you. (Psalm 32:8)

66 The Lord is good to everyone. He showers compassion on all his creation. (Psalms 145:9)

67 The Lord is righteous in everything he does; he is filled with kindness. (Psalms 145:17)

68 He will not let you stumble; the one who watches over you will not slumber. Indeed, he who watches over Israel never slumbers or sleeps. The Lord himself watches over you! The Lord stands beside you as your protective shade. The sun will not harm you by day, nor the moon at night. The Lord keeps you from all harm and watches over your life. The Lord keeps watch over you as you come and go, both now and forever. (Psalms 121:3-8)

69 For the Lord is the Spirit, and wherever the Spirit of the Lord is, there is freedom. (2 Corinthians 3:17)

70 You will keep in perfect peace all who trust in you, all whose thoughts are fixed on you! (Isaiah 26:3)

71 Taste and see that the Lord is good. Oh, the joys of those who take refuge in him! (Psalm 34:8)

72 I will teach you wisdom's ways and lead you in straight paths. (Proverbs 4:11)

73 He makes me as surefooted as a deer, enabling me to stand on mountain heights. (Psalms 18:33)

74 The Lord is my shepherd; I have all that I need. (Psalm 23:1)

75 God saved you by his grace when you believed. And you can't take credit for this; it is a gift from God. (Ephesians 2:8)

76 For the Lord your God is living among you. He is a mighty savior. He will take delight in you with gladness. With his love, he will calm all your fears. He will rejoice over you with joyful songs." (Zephaniah 3:17)

77 And I am certain that God, who began the good work within you, will continue his work until it is finally finished on the day when Christ Jesus returns. (Philippians 1:6)

78 The Lord is my shepherd; I have all that I need. He lets me rest in green meadows; he leads me beside peaceful streams. He renews my strength. He guides me along right paths, bringing honor to his name. (Psalm 23:1-3)

79 Give all your worries and cares to God, for he cares about you. (1 Peter 5:7)

80 Tozer, A. W. (2009). The Knowledge of the Holy: The Attributes of God: Their Meaning in the Christian Life (31935th ed.). HarperOne.

81 Judah said to his brothers, "What will we gain by killing our brother? We'd have to cover up the crime. Instead of hurting him, let's sell him to those Ishmaelite traders. After all, he is our brother—our own flesh and blood!" And his brothers agreed. So when the Ishmaelites, who were Midianite traders, came by, Joseph's brothers pulled him out of the cistern and sold him to them for twenty pieces[b] of silver. And the traders took him to Egypt. (Genesis 37:26-28)

82 So at last the king gave orders for Daniel to be arrested and thrown into the den of lions. The king said to him, "May your God, whom you serve so faithfully, rescue you." (Daniel 6:16)

83 So the next morning David wrote a letter to Joab and gave it to Uriah to deliver. The letter instructed Joab, "Station Uriah on the front lines where the battle is fiercest. Then pull back so that he will be killed." (2 Samuel 11:14-15)

84 The woman was surprised, for Jews refuse to have anything to do with Samaritans.[a] She said to Jesus, "You are a Jew, and I am a Samaritan woman. Why are you asking me for a drink?" Jesus replied, "If you only knew the gift God has for you and who you are speaking to, you would ask me, and I would give you living water." (John 4:9-10)

85 A woman in the crowd had suffered for twelve years with constant bleeding,[a] and she could find no cure. Coming up behind Jesus, she touched the fringe of his robe. Immediately, the bleeding stopped. (Luke 8:43-44)

86 Then he said to me, "Speak a prophetic message to these bones and say, 'Dry bones, listen to the word of the Lord! This is what the Sovereign Lord says: Look! I am going to put breath into you and make you live again! I will put flesh and muscles on you and cover you with skin. I will put breath into you, and you will come to life. Then you will know that I am the Lord.'" (Ezekiel 37:4-6)

87 The Lord is my shepherd; I have all that I need. He lets me rest in green meadows; he leads me beside peaceful streams. He renews my strength. He guides me along right paths, bringing honor to his name. Even when I walk through the darkest valley, I will not be afraid, for you are close beside me. Your rod and your staff protect and comfort me. You prepare a feast for me in the presence of my enemies. You honor me by anointing my head with oil. My cup overflows with blessings. Surely your goodness and unfailing love will pursue me all the days of my life, and I will live in the house of the Lord forever. (Psalm 23)

88 You will not leave in a hurry, running for your lives. For the Lord will go ahead of you; yes, the God of Israel will protect you from behind. (Isaiah 52:12)

89 For we are God's masterpiece. He has created us anew in Christ Jesus, so we can do the good things he planned for us long ago. (Ephesians 2:10)

90 And the Holy Spirit helps us in our weakness. For example, we don't know what God wants us to pray for. But the Holy Spirit prays for us with groanings that cannot be expressed in words. (Romans 8:26)

91 Take delight in the Lord, and he will give you your heart's desires. (Psalms 37:4)

92 Always be full of joy in the Lord. I say it again—rejoice! (Philippians 4:4)

93 Be thankful in all circumstances, for this is God's will for you who belong to Christ Jesus. (1 Thessalonians 5:18)

94 We love each other because he loved us first. (1 John 4:19)

95 You made all the delicate, inner parts of my body and knit me together in my mother's womb. (Psalms 139:13)

96 The thief's purpose is to steal and kill and destroy. My purpose is to give them a rich and satisfying life. (John 10:10)

97 And to the man he said, "Since you listened to your wife and ate from the tree whose fruit I commanded you not to eat, the ground is cursed because of you. All your life you will struggle to scratch a living from it. (Genesis 3:17)

After sending them out, the Lord God stationed mighty cherubim to the east of the Garden of Eden. And he placed a flaming sword that flashed back and forth to guard the way to the tree of life. (Genesis 3:24)

98 Jesus replied, "Anyone who drinks this water will soon become thirsty again. (John 4:13)

99 And I am convinced that nothing can ever separate us from God's love. Neither death nor life, neither angels nor demons,[a] neither our fears for today nor our worries about tomorrow—not even the powers of hell can separate us from God's love. (Romans 8:38)

100 "Be still, and know that I am God! I will be honored by every nation. I will be honored throughout the world." (Psalm 46:10)

101 Be still in the presence of the Lord, and wait patiently for him to act. Don't worry about evil people who prosper or fret about their wicked schemes. (Psalm 37:7)

102 Rejoice in our confident hope. Be patient in trouble, and keep on praying. (Romans 12:12)

103 So let's not get tired of doing what is good. At just the right time we will reap a harvest of blessing if we don't give up. (Galatians 6:9)

104 But if we look forward to something we don't yet have, we must wait patiently and confidently.) (Romans 8:25)

105 Those who have been ransomed by the Lord will return. They will enter Jerusalem singing, crowned with everlasting joy. Sorrow and mourning will disappear, and they will be filled with joy and gladness. (Isaiah 51:11)

106 The thief's purpose is to steal and kill and destroy. My purpose is to give them a rich and satisfying life. (John 10:10)

107 The Lord directs the steps of the godly. He delights in every detail of their lives. (Psalm 37:23)

108 Then Jesus said, "Come to me, all of you who are weary and carry heavy burdens, and I will give you rest. Take my yoke upon you. Let me teach you, because I am humble and gentle at heart, and you will find rest for your souls. For my yoke is easy to bear, and the burden I give you is light." (Matthew 11:28-30)

109 The thief's purpose is to steal and kill and destroy. My purpose is to give them a rich and satisfying life. (John 10:10)

110 Lewis, C. S. (2001). The Weight of Glory (1st ed.). HarperOne.

111 Jesus called a little child to him and put the child among them. Then he said, "I tell you the truth, unless you turn from your sins and become like little children, you will never get into the Kingdom of Heaven. So anyone who becomes as humble as this little child is the greatest in the Kingdom of Heaven. (Matt 18:2-4)

112 He must become greater and greater, and I must become less and less. (John 3:30)

113 Don't copy the behavior and customs of this world, but let God transform you into a new person by changing the way you think. Then you will learn to know God's will for you, which is good and pleasing and perfect. (Romans 12:2)

114 The Lord directs the steps of the godly. He delights in every detail of their lives. Though they stumble, they will never fall, for the Lord holds them by the hand. (Psalm 37:23-24)

115 For God made Christ, who never sinned, to be the offering for our sin,[a] so that we could be made right with God through Christ. (2 Corinthians 5:21)

116 Krulwich, R. (2011, November 18). Are You Totally Improbable Or Totally Inevitable? NPR. https://choice. npr.org/index.html?origin=https://www.npr.org/sections/ krulwich/2011/11/18/142513598/are-you-totally-improbable-or-totally-inevitable

117 "I knew you before I formed you in your mother's womb. Before you were born I set you apart and appointed you as my prophet to the nations." (Jeremiah 1:5)

118 You made all the delicate, inner parts of my body and knit me together in my mother's womb. (Psalms 139:13)

119 But to all who believed him and accepted him, he gave the right to become children of God. (John 1:12)

120 Then Jesus said, "Come to me, all of you who are weary and carry heavy burdens, and I will give you rest. 29 Take my yoke upon you. Let me teach you, because I am humble and gentle at heart, and you will find rest for your souls. 30 For my yoke is easy to bear, and the burden I give you is light." (Matthew 11:38-30)

121 God saved you by his grace when you believed. And you can't take credit for this; it is a gift from God. Salvation is not a reward for the good things we have done, so none of us can boast about it. (Ephesians 2:8-9)

122 "My thoughts are nothing like your thoughts," says the Lord. "And my ways are far beyond anything you could imagine. For just as the heavens are higher than the earth, so my ways are higher than your ways and my thoughts higher than your thoughts. (Isaiah 55: 8-9)

123 "My thoughts are nothing like your thoughts," says the Lord. "And my ways are far beyond anything you could imagine. For just as the heavens are higher than the earth, so my ways are higher than your ways and my thoughts higher than your thoughts. (Isaiah 55: 8-9)

124 He will wipe every tear from their eyes, and there will be no more death or sorrow or crying or pain. All these things are gone forever." (Revelation 21:4)

125 For we must all stand before Christ to be judged. We will each receive whatever we deserve for the good or evil we have done in this earthly body. (2 Corinthians 5:10)

126 Give your burdens to the Lord, and he will take care of you. He will not permit the godly to slip and fall. (Psalm 55:22)

127 For to me, living means living for Christ, and dying is even better. (Philippians 1:21)

128 He is so rich in kindness and grace that he purchased our freedom with the blood of his Son and forgave our sins. (Ephesians 1:7)

129 The angel who talked to me held in his hand a gold measuring stick to measure the city, its gates, and its wall. When he measured it, he found it was a square, as wide as it was long. In fact, its length and width and height were each 1,400 miles. Then he measured the walls and found them to be 216 feet thick (according to the human standard used by the angel). The wall was made of jasper, and the city was pure gold, as clear as glass. The wall of the city was built on foundation stones inlaid with twelve precious stones: the first was jasper, the second sapphire, the third agate, the fourth emerald, the fifth onyx, the sixth carnelian, the seventh chrysolite, the eighth beryl, the ninth topaz, the tenth chrysoprase, the eleventh jacinth, the twelfth amethyst. The twelve gates were made of pearls—each gate from a single pearl! And the main street was pure gold, as clear as glass. (Revelation 21: 15-21)

130 For to me, living means living for Christ, and dying is even better. (Philippians 1:21)

131 This is the day the Lord has made. We will rejoice and be glad in it. (Psalm 118:24)

132 On the day the Lord gave the Israelites victory over the Amorites, Joshua prayed to the Lord in front of all the people of Israel. He said, "Let the sun stand still over Gibeon, and the moon over the valley of Aijalon." So the sun stood still and the moon stayed in place until the nation of Israel had defeated its enemies. Is this event not recorded in The Book of Jashar? The sun stayed in the middle of the sky, and it did not set as on a normal day. There has never been a day like this one before or since, when the Lord answered such a prayer. Surely the Lord fought for Israel that day! (Joshua 10: 12-14)

133 Guard your heart above all else, for it determines the course of your life. (Proverbs 4:23)

134 For we are God's masterpiece. He has created us anew in Christ Jesus, so we can do the good things he planned for us long ago. (Ephesians 2:10)

135 I look up to the mountains— does my help come from there? (Psalm 121:1)

136 And this hope will not lead to disappointment. For we know how dearly God loves us, because he has given us the Holy Spirit to fill our hearts with his love. (Romans 5:5)

137 Then I heard the Lord asking, "Whom should I send as a messenger to this people? Who will go for us?" I said, "Here I am. Send me." (Isaiah 6:8)

138 You light a lamp for me. The Lord, my God, lights up my darkness. (Psalm 18:28)

139 Do not despise these small beginnings, for the Lord rejoices to see the work begin, to see the plumb line in Zerubbabel's hand." (The seven lamps[a] represent the eyes of the Lord that search all around the world.) (Zechariah 4:10)

140 "I am the Lord, and I do not change. That is why you descendants of Jacob are not already destroyed. (Malachi 3:6)

141 Then he told the people to sit down on the grass. Jesus took the five loaves and two fish, looked up toward heaven, and blessed them. Then, breaking the loaves into pieces, he gave the bread to the disciples, who distributed it to the people. They all ate as much as they wanted, and afterward, the disciples picked up twelve baskets of leftovers. About 5,000 men were fed that day, in addition to all the women and children! (Matthew 14:19-21)

142 The Lord told Gideon, "With these 300 men I will rescue you and give you victory over the Midianites. Send all the others home." (Judges 7:7)

143 Esther said, "If it please the king, and if I have found favor with him, and if he thinks it is right, and if I am pleasing to him, let there be a decree that reverses the orders of Haman son of Hammedatha the Agagite, who ordered that Jews throughout all the king's provinces should be destroyed. 6 For how can I endure to see my people and my family slaughtered and destroyed?" (Esther 8:5-6)

144 "You are the light of the world—like a city on a hilltop that cannot be hidden. (Matthew 5:14)

145 How sweet your words taste to me; they are sweeter than honey. (Psalm 119:103)

146 They are more desirable than gold, even the finest gold. They are sweeter than honey, even honey dripping from the comb. (Psalm 19:10)

147 Taste and see that the Lord is good. Oh, the joys of those who take refuge in him! (Psalm 34:8)

148 I pray that your hearts will be flooded with light so that you can understand the confident hope he has given to those he called— his holy people who are his rich and glorious inheritance. (Ephesians 1:18)

9 780578 943299